J 636.93583 SPA
Sparling, Rebecca.
Gerbils /

Gerbils

OUR BEST FRIENDS

OUR BEST FRIENDS

Gerbils

Rebecca Sparling

ELDORADO INK

Produced by OTTN Publishing, Stockton, New Jersey

Eldorado Ink
PO Box 100097
Pittsburgh, PA 15233
www.eldoradoink.com

First printing

1 3 5 7 9 8 6 4 2

Library of Congress Cataloging-in-Publication Data

Sparling, Rebecca.
  Gerbils / Rebecca Sparling.
      p. cm. — (Our best friends)
    ISBN 978-1-932904-28-4 (hardcover) — ISBN 978-1-932904-36-9 (trade edition)
    1. Gerbils as pets—Juvenile literature. 2. Gerbils—Juvenile literature. I. Title.
    SF459.G4S73 2008
    636.935'83—dc22

                          2008033058

Photo credits: Courtesy American Gerbil Society, 25; Zac Bowling,
www.flickr.com/photos/zbowling, 32, 38, 54; Courtesy Geodesic, www.flickr.com/photos/
geodesic, 49; © iStockphoto.com/Mark Hayes, 106; © iStockphoto.com/Bonita Hein, 91;
© iStockphoto.com/Erik Hougaard, 18, cover (middle inset); © iStockphoto.com/Thomas Peter,
11; © iStockphoto.com/Anneke Schram, 64; © iStockphoto.com/Matt Staples, 21, 35, 53 (gerbil); Conny Liegl, www.flickr.com/photos/moonsoleil, 59, 72; Diana Lili Meszaros, 41, 42; Katy
O'Neill, 45; Michael Pereckas, 30, 92; Courtesy Pet Sitters International, 96; Used under
license from Shutterstock, Inc., 3, 8, 13, 15, 16, 20, 23, 27, 29, 36, 44, 51, 53 (cat), 55, 58, 60,
62, 68, 69, 71, 74, 76, 77, 79, 82, 84, 85, 87, 88, 95, 97, 99, cover (main, top inset, bottom
inset, back cover), fun fact icon image (throughout).

TABLE OF CONTENTS

Introduction

The mutually beneficial relationship between humans and animals began long before the dawn of recorded history. Archaeologists believe that humans began to capture and tame wild goats, sheep, and pigs more than 9,000 years ago. These animals were then bred for specific purposes, such as providing humans with a reliable source of food or providing furs and hides that could be used for clothing or the construction of dwellings.

Other animals had been sought for companionship and assistance even earlier. The dog, believed to be the first animal domesticated, began living and working with Stone Age humans in Europe more than 14,000 years ago. Some archaeologists believe that wild dogs and humans were drawn together because both hunted the same prey. By taming and training dogs, humans became more effective hunters. Dogs, meanwhile, enjoyed the social contact with humans and benefited from greater access to food and warm shelter. Dogs soon became beloved pets as well as trusted workers. This can be seen from the many artifacts depicting dogs that have been found at ancient sites in Asia, Europe, North America, and the Middle East.

The earliest domestic cats appeared in the Middle East about 5,000 years ago. Small wild cats were probably first attracted to human settlements because plenty of rodents could be found wherever harvested grain was stored. Cats played a useful role in hunting and killing these pests, and it is likely that grateful humans rewarded them for this assistance. Over time, these small cats gave up some of their aggressive wild behaviors and began living among humans. Cats eventually became so popular in ancient Egypt that they were believed to possess magical powers. Cat statues were placed outside homes to ward off evil spirits, and mummified cats were included in royal tombs to accompany their owners into the afterlife.

Today, few people believe that cats have supernatural powers, but most pet owners feel a magical bond with their pets, whether they are dogs, cats, hamsters, rabbits, horses, or parrots. The lives of pets and their people become inextricably intertwined, providing strong emotional and physical rewards for both humans and animals. People of all ages can benefit from the loving companionship of a pet. Not surprisingly, then, pet ownership is widespread. Recent statistics indicate that about 60 percent of all households in the United States and Canada have at least one pet, while the figure is close to 50 percent of households in the United Kingdom. For millions of people, therefore, pets truly have become their "best friends."

Finding the best animal friend can be a challenge, however. Not only are there many types of domesticated pets, but each has specific needs, characteristics, and personality traits. Even within a category of pets, such as dogs, different breeds will flourish in different surroundings and with different treatment. For example, a German Shepherd may not be the right pet for a person living in a cramped urban apartment; that person might be better off caring for a smaller dog like a Toy Poodle or Shih Tzu, or perhaps a cat. On the other hand, an active person who loves the outdoors may prefer the companion-

ship of a Labrador Retriever to that of a small dog or a passive indoor pet like a goldfish or hamster.

The joys of pet ownership come with certain responsibilities. Bringing a pet into your home and your neighborhood obligates you to care for and train the pet properly. For example, a dog must be housebroken, taught to obey your commands, and trained to behave appropriately when he encounters other people or animals. Owners must also be mindful of their pet's particular nutritional and medical needs.

The purpose of the OUR BEST FRIENDS series is to provide a helpful and comprehensive introduction to pet ownership. Each book contains the basic information a prospective pet owner needs in order to choose the right pet for his or her situation and to care for that pet throughout the pet's lifetime. Training, socialization, proper nutrition, potential medical issues, and the legal responsibilities of pet ownership are thoroughly explained and discussed, and an abundance of expert tips and suggestions are offered. Whether it is a hamster, corn snake, guinea pig, or Labrador Retriever, the books in the OUR BEST FRIENDS series provide everything the reader needs to know about how to have a happy, well-adjusted, and well-behaved pet.

Gerbils are fascinating creatures. They make interesting pets for children because they are fun to watch and don't mind being handled.

CHAPTER ONE

Are Gerbils Right for You?

Gerbils make great pets. They are cute little daredevils that are fun to watch, and they have snuggly bodies and enjoy cozying up with each other—and occasionally their human owners. They also take up minimal space, make little noise, and do not smell too much if they are cared for properly. Although gerbils are terrific for children, kids still need guidance from adults to care for them correctly. Remember that gerbils can live up to five years, so you should be sure you are ready to commit that kind of time to them before purchasing gerbils.

Gerbils are social creatures that enjoy being together. In fact, they really do not like to be alone. Lonely gerbils tend to live short, unhealthy lives. Therefore, many gerbil experts recommend that you keep at least two gerbils.

Gerbils look like fuzzy little mice, but they are larger than mice and smaller than rats. The shape of their faces is slightly different from that of mice and rats. Gerbils weigh about two to four ounces (57–113 g). Adults are about five inches (13 cm) long, but they also have furry tails that are just as long as their bodies and end with a little tuft of hair. Domesticated gerbils come in an array of colors, such as brown, white, black, orange, gold, red, slate, and any mix of those colors. Most gerbils' fur is some form of agouti—a

FAST FACT

Gerbils make great pets for people who suffer from asthma and cannot have pet cats or dogs.

color that is very similar to the color of common wild rabbits. Gerbils can have black, red, or pink eyes.

GERBIL BEHAVIOR

Gerbils love to exercise! They are naturally active. They often sprint across their cage or dart out of a hiding place and surprise you. Gerbils are generally skittish, but those that are always treated kindly will usually learn to trust their owners. Gerbils will often stand on their hind legs and observe their surroundings. Some gerbils can be taught tricks, such as running up a person's arm or sitting on top of a person's head.

Gerbils will often be up and about all day and night because they sleep only for about two to four hours at a time and stay awake for the same duration. Gerbils are not nocturnal: Nocturnal animals sleep during the daytime and are active at night. Gerbils are sometimes diurnal: Diurnal animals sleep at night and are active during the daytime. Gerbils are primarily crepuscular, which

means that they are active during the twilight and dawn hours of a day. In the wild, most gerbils live in Central Asia, where they must survive cold winters and hot summers. Keeping a crepuscular schedule allows gerbils to find food and water during the hours when temperatures are moderate. Then the gerbils stay in their burrows and sleep for the very hot and cold hours of the day.

Gerbils spend a lot of time building and maintaining their nests. When gerbils are improving an existing nest, they work on their own. When gerbils need to build a nest from scratch, adult gerbils will band together to complete the nest. All gerbils enjoy digging through their bedding. They also dig in the corners of their cages, a practice which is called burrowing.

Gerbils love to gnaw on untreated wood and thin cardboard. This is natural; a gerbil's teeth grow constantly, so gnawing prevents their teeth from getting too long. As a result, though you'll find that you need to regularly replace your gerbils' chew toys. If one of your gerbils chews on the bars of a metal cage, it might be bored. In this case, your gerbil may need some more things to do. If you pre-cut some round holes in a piece of untreated wood that measures 4 inches by 4 inches, it can

Your gerbil will amuse himself for hours by chewing a piece of cardboard or wood. Chewing is normal and natural for gerbils, and helps to keep their teeth trimmed to the proper length.

serve double duty as a chewing post and a jungle gym.

Gerbils have scent glands on their bellies, and they often rub their bellies against things to leave their scents behind. This behavior is called marking, because gerbils are marking their territory and anything they would like to claim as their own.

Gerbils commonly fight with each other, but they are usually only having fun. Many gerbils engage in play fighting, but this can get out of hand. Watch closely to make sure that your

FAST FACT

Gerbils exchange greetings by running up to each other and rubbing noses. Some gerbils have even been known to rub noses with their humans.

gerbils are not having a serious fight. If they appear to be hurting each other, or if one is clearly unable to defend itself, you should separate the gerbils. If you see bite marks on one of your gerbils or notice that it refuses to sleep in the nest, you should assume that this gerbil is at risk of being in a serious fight. Gerbils that fight in anger have been known to seriously injure and even kill their opponents. Gerbils often chatter their teeth to signal that they are angry, so be on the alert for this telltale sign that your gerbils are truly angry, and not just kidding around.

Another habit of gerbils is thumping—they thump their hind legs on the ground. Gerbils thump when they feel their colony is under attack—or when one gerbil and its mate feel threatened. They also thump when they are sexually aroused. If your gerbils live in multiple tanks, one gerbil may thump for a while until a gerbil in another tank thumps back.

Gerbils spend a lot of time grooming each other. Grooming is more than just keeping each other clean—it is also a sign of companionship among gerbils. Another way they stay clean is by taking dust baths. You should provide a dust bath in your gerbil's cage because a dust bath will keep your gerbils clean and healthy. Chapter 5 will explain the proper way to set up a dust bath.

Gerbils also commonly escape. Gerbils love to find undiscovered holes, crawl through them, and explore the world outside their cage. They are extremely clever, so you will need a good lid on your cage. If your gerbils go missing from their cage, you should secure other pets, like cats and dogs: They could find your gerbils before you do—with tragic results for the gerbils. Gerbils do not usually stray very far from home, and if they can, they may just crawl back to their tank when they

FAST FACT

Gerbils that are only six to eight weeks old do not usually have a problem getting along with another gerbil, but older gerbils need to be introduced to each other slowly because they may attack gerbils that have a foreign scent.

get hungry. Chapter 4 will give you some tips to finding your gerbils if they escape.

EATING AND DRINKING

Gerbils eat mostly grains and seeds, but they also enjoy green plants, fruit, and insects. Gerbils do not drink much water; for that reason, they do not produce much urine. Gerbils do require a non-drip water bottle in their tanks at all times. Even though they will not drink much water, they should always have clean, fresh water available.

Premixed gerbil food is available in most pet stores. These premixed foods will help your gerbils get the correct mix of nutrients they need. Some premixed foods have sunflower seeds in them. Sunflower seeds are very fattening for gerbils, so if your gerbils are a little overweight, you may want to pick out most of the sunflower seeds before serving the premixed food.

Gerbil food can be purchased from your local pet store. Be sure to check that the packaging is firmly sealed, to ensure its freshness.

GERBIL ANCESTRY

The first known gerbils to be bred by humans were a group of twenty pairs caught in 1935 in the Amur River basin in eastern Mongolia. Taken to a laboratory in Japan for use in medical testing, these gerbils bred and produced pups that were sent to countries all over the world, as testing subjects and then also as pets. The first gerbils bred in the United States were descendants of these pups. It is widely believed that most of today's commercially bred gerbils are, too.

In 1995, scientists captured wild Mongolian gerbils to compare them to domesticated gerbils. Keeping gerbils as pets seems to have changed their physiology. Scientists found that wild gerbils are smaller than gerbils bred in captivity. Gerbils in captivity have smaller brains and learn differently than wild gerbils. While wild gerbils breed only during certain times of the year, gerbils in captivity breed throughout the year. Some captive gerbils also suffer from occasional seizures, while wild gerbils do not seem to be subject to these same seizures.

Your gerbils will eat from a food dish, but they will most likely hide their food in their bedding. This is the gerbil's way of keeping its food safe from other gerbils. A food dish will help prevent your gerbil's food from becoming contaminated. Gerbils often hold their food when they eat. You may notice them standing on their hind legs while holding a nut or seed with their front paws.

They will also turn the food when they want to chomp on the other side. When they are finished eating, the gerbils will leave any inedible husks on the ground and go find something else to do.

NATURAL HABITAT

Before gerbils became popular American pets, they were desert creatures thriving in the sands of Mongolia. Gerbils hail from the Steppes—the semi-arid, grass-covered plains of Mongolia in Central Asia. Gerbils were first discovered in China in the early 1900s. In the wild, gerbils live in family groups, called clans or colonies. Most gerbil

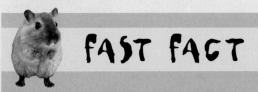

FAST FACT

The correct term for a baby gerbil is *pup*.

The gerbils kept as pets in the United States, Canada, and the United Kingdom are descended from wild gerbils native to the deserts of Mongolia.

families reside together, and they recognize each other by smell. To build that smell, they lick other gerbils in their families and coat their family in a layer of saliva. Ten to fifteen gerbils usually make up a colony. If there are more gerbils than that in a colony, fights tend to break out.

In the wild, gerbils burrow in the sand to protect themselves. Wild gerbils have adapted to the extreme temperatures of Mongolia. They deal with intense heat and cold by

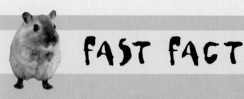

FAST FACT

Dilute gerbils are very rare. They are available in various blue shades.

In the wild, gerbils subsist on seeds, plants, and insects. Pet gerbils will be happy if you supplement their seed mix with lettuce, carrots, and other vegetables they can chew.

burrowing and hiding away. Gerbil colonies construct complicated tunnel systems underground, and they defend their clans from neighboring gerbil colonies.

Gerbils are monogamous and mate for life. One male and female couple mate, and their brothers and sisters help raise the pups. If a helper gerbil wants to produce offspring, it will leave its established group to find a mate and start its own family.

Wild gerbils eat roots, flowers, seeds, and plants. Their natural habitat is dry, so not many predators can live there. For this reason, they are adept at protecting themselves only from other gerbils.

In the 1950s, American scientists began to use gerbils in laboratory experiments. Legend has it that some members of the laboratory staff fell in love with the fuzzy little creatures and began taking them home to their children as pets. In the early 1960s, gerbils began appearing at pet stores in the United States.

THE COST OF YOUR GERBILS

Chapter 4 will give you specific details on the supplies and housing you will need to buy for your gerbils. The cage or tank is usually the most expensive piece of gerbil equipment. In purchasing gerbils, you will probably incur a one-time cost of about $120. Gerbils cost, on average, about $10 each. Other one-time costs include the gerbil's cage, food dish, water bottle, and toys. Gerbils also require things that have to be replaced regularly, such as food, fresh veggies and fruit, and bedding. You may also need to take your gerbils to a veterinarian annually. It costs about $200 a year to keep gerbils.

CHAPTER TWO

Finding the Right Gerbils

Gerbils look similar to mice, rats, and hamsters. Gerbils are larger than mice and smaller than rats, and they have tails, while hamsters do not. These similarities in appearance occur because gerbils—members of the *gerbillinae* family—belong to the same suborder as mice and rats—these small rodents are all cousins. Scientists have identified at least eighty species of gerbils, many of which live in dry, hot desert climates

Although Mongolian gerbils are the most common, a variety of gerbils are kept as pets.

in Africa, Europe, and Asia. Pet gerbils are usually Mongolian gerbils, but occasionally, fat-tailed duprasis, pallid gerbils, Persian jirds, and Shaw's jirds are kept as pets. You should never house different species of gerbils together because they would fight.

Before you start learning about gerbils, you should learn to identify gerbils by their Latin names. These Latin names are made of two different parts. The first part is the genus name, and the second part is the species name. These scientific, Latin names are useful when researching or buying different species of gerbils. If you want to find information about gerbils, common names are unreliable. These common regional or local nicknames often differ slightly, and they sometimes refer to more than one animal. One animal also might have more than one common name. The Mongolian gerbil, for example, has many different common names such as the Mongolian desert gerbil and the clawed gerbil. It has, however, only one scientific name—*Meriones unguiculatus*. This might seem like a mouthful, but if you are trying to find information about this species, it is useful to know the scientific, Latin name.

Northern and southern pygmy gerbils belong to the genus *Gerbillus*. Large naked-sole gerbils belong to the genus *Tatera*, and small naked-sole gerbils belong to the genus *Taterillus*. Jirds belong to the genus *Meriones*. Mongolian gerbils—the gerbils most commonly kept as pets—belong to the jird grouping, which are found naturally in Central Asia. These gerbils are used to the extremely hot summers and very cold winters of Mongolia and northeastern China.

Mongolian gerbils are the most common pet gerbils, so it is easiest to find information about the housing, nutritional, and breeding needs of this species. If you decide to get a different species of gerbil, however, you will have to research the specific species that you choose. The Internet is a good place to look for information about specific species of gerbils. You can also visit a library or pet store to find books and articles about different species of gerbils. Pet store employees and gerbil breeders usually

FAST FACT

The scientific name for the Mongolian gerbil—*Meriones unguiculatus*—comes from *Meriones*, which is Greek for "warrior," and *unguiculatus*, which is Latin for "with claws." This furry gerbil's name literally means "warrior with claws"!

Gerbils are not solitary animals. If you're thinking of getting one, consider getting two so that your little friend isn't lonely.

provide the best information about the needs of your gerbils' species.

HOW MANY GERBILS TO GET

Before you try to pick out gerbils, you have to make a few decisions. You should always keep at least a pair of gerbils. Gerbils are not solitary creatures. They are not happy by themselves, so if you keep one gerbil, it could become lonely or sick and even die. Gerbils are extremely social and need a companion for security, grooming, and warmth. Lonely gerbils are likely to become irritable, nervous, lethargic, and obese. To keep your gerbils as healthy and happy as possible, you need to have two gerbils. Before simply choosing two gerbils, however, you must consider that a male gerbil and a female gerbil together will mate constantly. Gerbil pups are cute, so this may seem like a good idea, but it is also a lot of work. Each pair of gerbils will produce a new litter of pups every thirty to forty days. A female gerbil's reproductive life lasts about a year and a half—this means your gerbils could produce six or seven litters, taking into account days spent nursing. The average litter of gerbil pups is four to six pups, but gerbils have been known to have as many as twelve pups in a litter. This could get to be a huge number of gerbil pups!

If you plan to breed gerbils, you should be aware that it takes a great deal of work. Finding new homes for all the gerbils will be a difficult task. Pet stores are not always interested in taking weaned pups, so you may have to find individual homes for each pup. The best approach to breeding gerbils is to get two gerbils that are unusual colors or different species. Pet stores may be more likely to take pups produced by these gerbils.

If you do not plan to breed gerbils, you should purchase either two male gerbils or two female gerbils. Some experts think two male gerbils get along better, while others think two female gerbils do; it is widely believed, however, that female gerbils get meaner as they get older. Assuming that you would still rather adopt a male and a female gerbil, look for a veterinarian who will spay and neuter your gerbils. This would

If you do decide to get two or more gerbils, they should all be approximately the same age. Young gerbils will form a stronger bond if they grow up together.

prevent your gerbils from breeding. Although female gerbils can be spayed and male gerbils can be neutered, this procedure is rare, so it might be difficult for you to find a veterinarian qualified to perform the surgery. You can contact a local humane or gerbil society to see if any veterinarians in your area perform this procedure.

When you buy your gerbils, you should buy them both at the same time, and you should buy two young gerbils. This will allow your gerbils to grow up together, to bond with each other, which will prevent them from fighting. Older gerbils can become territorial, and introducing a new gerbil into this environment could cause your gerbils to fight with each other. If you have to introduce one gerbil, a male gerbil is easier to introduce—especially to a pup. If you buy a pair of young gerbils at the same time, they will bond with each other. They may wrestle with or chase each other, but this will be play fighting, which is a sign of affection among your gerbils. As long as your gerbils are not injuring each other, this play fighting is fine. Your gerbils will also groom each other, sleep together, and cuddle.

As a beginner to gerbil keeping, you should not house more than two gerbils together in one cage. If you do, a pair of gerbils will form a closer bond, and they will pick on the odd gerbil out. This could cause problems. Keeping more than one pair of gerbils in the same cage may also cause gerbils to fight with each other. Some people have been known to house colonies of ten to fifteen gerbils together, but this is not recommended for beginners.

MALE OR FEMALE GERBILS

After you decide whether you want a male gerbil and a female gerbil, two male gerbils, or two female gerbils, you will need to choose these gerbils. This means you will have to learn to tell them apart. Some people claim that female gerbils are more active and curious than male gerbils are, but this is not a scientific way to determine the sex of gerbils. Male gerbils are generally larger than female gerbils. They also have a stronger scent than female gerbils. If the gerbils are kept in a clean cage, however, this odor cannot be easily detected.

To determine a gerbil's sex accurately, you have to examine it closely. You can tell a young male gerbil apart from a female gerbil by the dark-colored scrotum near the base of its tail. It is easier to tell adult gerbils apart this way—telling the difference in young gerbils is very difficult.

When you buy younger gerbils, you will have to compare them in a cage. You should look at the distance between the anus and the genital papilla. This distance is much larger in male gerbils than in female gerbils. Male gerbils will also have some swelling near the scrotum. Female gerbils will have nipples, but it can be very hard to see them. You may want to blow gently on the gerbil's belly. This could part the hair enough to see nipples in a female.

Remember that gerbils can begin breeding as young as eight to twelve weeks old. So if a female gerbil is not separated early enough from male gerbils, she could be pregnant by the time you make your purchase. You should try to buy your gerbil from a store or organization that keeps male and female gerbils separated. You can also ask how old the gerbils are. This may help you to make an educated guess about whether your female gerbil might be pregnant.

YOUNG OR OLDER?

When choosing gerbils, you will have to decide whether you want to purchase young gerbils or older gerbils. At twelve weeks old, gerbils are considered adults. Between three and four weeks old, gerbils are weaned. You should not buy a pup that was just weaned. Weaning is a stressful time for a young pup, and moving to a new home is equally as stressful. These combined stressors can cause a young gerbil to become sick. In the five-to-eight-week-old range, gerbils are ready for their new homes. Their bodies are between two and three inches long (5–7.5 cm) at this age.

For beginners to gerbil keeping, it is best to start with younger gerbils. At six to eight weeks old, gerbils are extremely easy to place together. They are young enough to form a close bond. It is more difficult to get older gerbils to form a bond. If you have to introduce two older gerbils, you should be careful and watch them closely. Chapter 4 will present a plan to introduce gerbils to each other.

Gerbils make great pets whether they are older or younger.

You should choose two gerbils that are about the same age. Gerbils become sad and lonely when one of a pair passes away, so choosing gerbils of the same age is important. This ensures that your gerbils will be able to spend as much time together as possible.

Younger gerbils are also easier to tame. If you choose older gerbils that have been handled infrequently, they may be unfriendly. You can handle young gerbils frequently and raise them to be good pets.

WHERE TO GET YOUR GERBILS

Once you have decided to get gerbils, how many gerbils you want, whether you want male or female gerbils, and how old your gerbils will be, you should establish your gerbils' new home before purchasing these furry pets. Chapter 4 will give you more information about the supplies you will need before bringing gerbils into your house and about how to set up your gerbils' living space. After your gerbils' home is prepared, you are finally ready to buy your new gerbils.

PET STORES: A clean, well-kept pet store is a good place to buy gerbils. Pet stores often carry many supplies for gerbils, such as housing, bedding, food, and toys. Generally speaking, the employees at a local pet store are knowledgeable about the nutrition and housing needs of the animals they sell. This means that the pet store employees can give you advice about caring for your gerbils. The employees can also help you determine the sex of your young gerbils.

It is important, however, to buy your gerbils at a reputable pet store. Since pet stores are commercial, some of them are more concerned about making money than about properly caring for their animals. Before purchasing a gerbil at the local pet store, you should see if local gerbil societies and veterinarians in your area recommend that pet store. You can also ask other gerbil owners whether they would recommend a particular store. You should always make sure the

 FAST FACT

Pet stores usually do not stock a variety of colors and species of gerbils. If you are looking for a particular species or color, however, the local pet store may be able to special order it for you. Before you exercise this option, though, keep in mind that you will not be able to observe the behavior and environment of special-ordered gerbils before they become yours.

The Web site of the American Gerbil Society (AGS) includes a registry of breeders, organized by state. It is available at www.agsgerbils.org/Breeders.html.

store is clean, and you should obtain at least two recommendations before purchasing from a pet store.

BREEDERS: Gerbil breeders are generally people who love gerbils, and run their operations based on that approach, rather than as commercial businesses. This means that most—though not all—breeders take exceptional care of their gerbils. Breeders often sell their gerbils at a price comparable to pet stores. Before choosing to purchase your gerbil from a particular breeder, make sure the breeder's gerbils seem to be well cared for and kept in a clean environment. You should contact local gerbil

societies and veterinarians in your area to obtain recommendations for gerbil breeders. It is wise to get at least two recommendations from veterinarians, friends, or gerbil owners before buying from a particular breeder. You can also check to see if the gerbil breeder is licensed through the American Gerbil Society (AGS).

Remember, too, that if you get gerbils from a breeder who breeds large numbers of gerbils, your gerbils may not be as friendly or tame as gerbils bred by hobbyists who care for fewer gerbils. If breeders have a large number of gerbils at one time, they do not usually have a lot of time to dedicate to taming each individual gerbil. Therefore, with this kind of breeding operation, you may have a harder time finding a gerbil with a gentle, friendly temperament.

You can also try to find an AGS-licensed breeder outside your area. If you are willing to travel to purchase your gerbil, this might be a good idea. If you do not plan on traveling, however, it may be difficult to get a gerbil from a distant breeder. It is illegal to ship gerbils via the U.S. Postal Service. Some airlines will agree to ship your gerbils, but this could be stressful and dangerous for your gerbils. If you decide to have your gerbils shipped to you on an airplane, you have to guarantee safe,

YOUR GERBIL SEARCH

You can sometimes find pet gerbils listed in your local classified ads. The local newspaper often has a pets section where you might be able to find supplies and housing for your gerbils as well. If you cannot find the gerbils you want, the Internet is also a valuable tool. The Internet can link you to many different Web sites to help you find the pet you are looking for. Petfinder.com enables people to find pets that are up for adoption from rescues and shelters. The American Gerbil Society (AGS) also has its own classified section.

appropriate conditions for your gerbils. Certain airlines will allow small pets like gerbils to travel in a plane's main cabin, if they are secured in a carrier and have appropriate health documents. Contact a reputable, professional pet transportation company to arrange a safe trip for the gerbils. (The Web site www. petsonthego.com lists many of these organizations.)

RESCUES OR SHELTERS: Another option for getting gerbils is to adopt them from a rescue or animal shelter. Local humane societies often accept small animals, such as hamsters and gerbils, whose owners can no longer care for them. There are rescues that specialize in saving unwanted gerbils, but you may also be able to find gerbils at other animal rescues and shelters. If you get gerbils through a shelter or rescue, you are giving a good home to gerbils that need one. You should remember, however, that these gerbils might have been neglected or even mistreated. They may not have friendly temperaments; they may even be mean. You should consider whether you have the time and commitment it takes to tame unfriendly gerbils. This job may be better suited to someone with a great deal of experience with gerbils. You also may not be able to accurately determine the age of a gerbil you are considering adopting from a shelter or rescue.

CHOOSING HEALTHY GERBILS

Wherever you decide to get your gerbils, you should always make sure they come from clean, healthy conditions. Gerbils produce an odor, so some smell is normal. A strong smell, however, is a sign of poor care. If the gerbils have an empty food dish or water bottle, the gerbils are probably

Your local humane society or animal shelter may have a gerbil or two that are looking for a good home.

poorly cared for. These are signs that you are getting unhealthy, unhappy gerbils. If any breeder, pet store, or shelter is keeping gerbils in these conditions, you should refuse to purchase any gerbils from them.

Even if you think you might like a particular gerbil, you do not want to buy a gerbil that will become sick and die. If a cage is dirty or over-crowded, or if a gerbil in a cage is ill, you should not buy any gerbils from that place. What if the gerbils you like are not exhibiting symp-toms of illness? You should not buy gerbils from any cage that contains sick gerbils. Why not? Because all the gerbils in the cage have been exposed to illness, and the stress of moving to a new home could cause a gerbil kept in those conditions to get sick. When you look for signs of healthy, happy gerbils, look for these signs in all the gerbils in a cage—not just the gerbils you plan to purchase.

WHAT YOUR GERBILS SHOULD LOOK LIKE

After you have decided where you are going to purchase your gerbils, spend some time observing how the gerbils look and behave. You want to make sure you are getting friendly, happy, and healthy pet gerbils. So carefully examine how your prospec-tive gerbils look and how they inter-act with others.

Healthy gerbils have dense, shiny coats of fur. The fur should be smooth and sleek. If any gerbil in a cage has bald patches or flaky skin, you should not purchase gerbils from that cage. You should also check that the gerbils do not have scabs or lumps on their skin. Never purchase gerbils with rough or thin coats of fur. This could be from poor care or from an infection or illness. Never purchase thin, frail-looking gerbils, either. Your gerbils should be solid and plump, but not overweight.

Look closely at the gerbils' eyes before buying them. Their eyes should be bright and clear. The nose on each one should be free of dis-charge. Runny eyes or a runny nose are signs of a problem. The gerbils should not be sneezing or unrespon-sive. A sick gerbil wipes its runny nose and eyes on its front feet. Check the gerbils' front feet to make sure the fur there is not wet or mat-ted. This is a sign of an illness. If the fur near the tail is dirty or matted, this could indicate that the gerbil has diarrhea.

To make sure your gerbils are healthy, watch how they walk. You should not buy gerbils that are limp-ing or moving strangely. Look at each gerbil's tail—gerbils that are missing parts of their tail may have been improperly cared for. Sometimes a gerbil loses a piece of its tail because the tail got caught in an exercise wheel, but this is less likely when appropriate exercise wheels are provided. A tail with a slight kink in it may have been inherited. Although this is not good for show gerbils, it will not make your gerbils any less prized as great pets. Gerbils with damaged tails can still be healthy, be happy, and live long, normal lives.

HOW YOUR GERBILS SHOULD BEHAVE

In addition to carefully examining the appearance of your gerbils, closely observe their behavior to make sure they are healthy, happy, and docile. If you can, spend some time just watching gerbils at different breeders, pet stores, and shelters before making your final decisions. You should buy gerbils only if you are allowed to handle them first to ensure that they are friendly and have gentle temperaments.

If your gerbil's fur appears matted or thin, it may be a sign of a health problem.

FAST FACT

Gerbils communicate by squeaking and thumping their back legs. Sometimes gerbils make an odd, ultrasonic sound to communicate with one another.

Getting gerbils with friendly dispositions and good personalities is important.

Some gerbils are friendly, calm, and gentle, while others are nervous

When choosing a pet, look for a gerbil that is not afraid of being held. Your gerbils should be curious and interested in exploring their surroundings.

and excitable. Friendly, calm gerbils are obviously better choices as pets, but sometimes skittish, nervous gerbils can be tamed. Proper breeding, appropriate care, and a clean, suitable environment all affect gerbils' personalities. You can tame gerbils by playing with them often and pro-

viding them with a good home. Although these things will increase your chance of getting good pets, you should also seek out gerbils that exhibit certain behaviors.

When you are buying gerbils, you should choose gerbils that are curious and responsive. Healthy, happy gerbils will investigate when their cage is opened or when you place your hand into their cage. If a particular gerbil crawls onto your hand, this bold, curious gerbil is a great choice as a pet. If a gerbil sniffs your hand, runs away, and comes back, this gerbil would also make a good pet. Gerbils sometimes nip with their teeth—this will not hurt or draw blood, though it may startle you. You should never choose a gerbil that runs away and hides, is aggressive toward you or other gerbils, or tries to bite. If you

FAST FACT

Gerbils sniff noses and mouths, and nudge bodies and behinds, to communicate with other gerbils from their clan. Even in the wild, gerbils will groom each other.

try to hold a particular gerbil and it frantically squirms to get away, this gerbil is a bad choice as a pet. Once you think you have found the right gerbils, you are ready to take them home!

CHAPTER THREE

Responsible Gerbil Ownership

One of the most rewarding and the most difficult choices that gerbil owners make is the decision to breed. Female gerbils reach sexual maturity at around two to three months of age. From that point on, a pair of gerbils will produce a new litter every thirty to forty days for about a year and a half. This could result in over a hundred gerbil pups in the lifetime of a mating pair. This is why it is extremely important to know the sex of your gerbils before purchasing them.

Of course, the unexpected may occur, despite your best efforts. You might look in the tank one day and discover several small, pink creatures

The male gerbil plays an important role in caring for pups.

squeaking loudly. If you purchased a pair of female gerbils, one or both of them most likely became pregnant at the pet store. This can happen when housing females older than seven or eight weeks with adult male gerbils. The first thing you should do is determine which gerbil is the mom. Watch your gerbils to see which one nurses and cares for the babies—that is the pups' mother. Once you know who the mom is, remove the other female from the tank. Two female gerbils will not get along once pups are part of the picture. The mother will view the other female as a threat to her pups. The mom may lash out at her former friend, or the other female may attack the pups. Leave the mother and the pups in the original tank, and make a new home for the other female. (If the second female also happens to be pregnant, follow the same procedure for her and her pups.) After weaning and separating the pups from the mother (or mothers), you might try reintroducing the two adult females. This process can be difficult. Until your gerbils become reacquainted, be sure to start slowly, using the split cage method described in Chapter 4.

Alternatively, one of the two gerbils you thought was female could turn out to be male. If this is the case, you should consider leaving mom and dad together. Gerbils form a very close bond to their mates. Separating a mother gerbil from her mate could cause stress and lead her to neglect her pups. Male gerbils make great fathers. They assist the mother in keeping the pups warm and grooming. Males also make mother gerbils feel protected during this very stressful period. Instead of removing the male from the tank, there are several options to consider if you do not wish to continue breeding. First, it is important to know that gerbils mate during or immediately after the birthing process. If the litter was a complete surprise, you can bet that your female is already pregnant with another set of pups. Your female gerbil will not give birth again until she weans the current litter, however. This will most

FAST FACT

Although most gerbil births go very smoothly, you may want to put together an emergency birthing kit. Your emergency kit should contain a clamp lamp and a warming light; powdered kitten replacement milk; Ornacycline antibiotic, which can be found in pet stores; and emergency contact numbers of your local veterinarian and local gerbil breeders.

likely delay the birth of the second litter by forty days. During this time, you will have to decide what to with the male.

If you do not wish to split up the male and female, you can have the male neutered to prevent future pregnancies. This practice is not common in smaller animals, so finding a veterinarian willing and able to perform the procedure might be difficult. (It is possible to spay a female gerbil, but this complicated surgery is even less common than neutering.) Another option involves separating mom and dad after weaning the current litter. In that case, leave one of the daughters with the mother gerbil to help care for the new pups that will arrive shortly. You should put the father gerbil and one of the sons in a separate tank to prevent the older male from becoming lonely. If you do not wish to care for the other pups, be sure to find them good homes with responsible gerbil owners. It may also be a good idea to spread the word to other owners that you have another litter on the way. This could help you find appropriate homes for the pups in the second litter.

PLANNED PARENTHOOD

Breeding gerbils is an expensive, time-consuming, and frustrating undertaking. If you are a beginner, it is best not to consider gerbil breeding. You should stick to raising adult pairs for a while. After caring for several sets of gerbils, you may decide that breeding is something you are interested in doing. There are several things to consider before breeding. Ask yourself if you realistically have the time to dedicate to breeding. Once your breeding pair has produced a litter, the breeder has to raise friendly, tame gerbils. This takes a lot of time and patience. Breeding also requires a great deal of space. You need to have enough room for several tanks or cages to house separate litters once the mother weans them. In addition, assess the market for gerbils in your area. If there are many pet stores in your region, that might indicate a demand for small animals like gerbils. You should also be aware that breeders do not make a lot of money from the pups they sell. Breeding should be done out of love for the species and not as a way to make money.

The first step in gerbil breeding is to select the mating pair. You may want to obtain your gerbils from a local breeder. A breeder will have crucial knowledge about the health and temperament of a specific line of gerbils. Pet store employees are not likely to have this type of information. There are three factors to con-

Before breeding your gerbils, why not spend time with the gerbils you have. Owning just two may be enough responsibility.

sider when choosing a breeding pair—health, temperament, and color. Be sure to ask the breeder if the parents in this breeding line have produced any litters with runts or pups with respiratory infections. Find out if any of the pups produced in this line have had genetic defects, such as kinked tails or seizure disorders. It is not a good idea to breed from a line that has experienced these problems. The goal of breeding is to strengthen the species. This is why it is important to select the strongest, healthiest gerbils for your mating pair.

Learn all you can about the temperament of the parents in the breeding line. Question the breeder about how the parents interact with their pups. You want to know that your gerbils have come from a line of attentive, nurturing parents. It is also crucial to know how the parents interact with people. It is easier to find good homes for friendly gerbils.

The final consideration is the color. As discussed earlier, gerbils with unusual coats are in higher demand than gerbils with plain coats. Pups with spotting, rich colors, and color points are much easier to place. Learning a little about gerbil genetics will help you determine what color pups a pair might produce.

After you have selected your breeding pair, introduce them slowly and carefully. Chapter 4 will describe how to introduce gerbils. Once your gerbils have an established bond, place them in a tank away from any loud noises or other animals. Stress can affect your gerbils' ability to breed. Keep the tank simple. You should avoid any levels, ladders, toys, or tubes. These items could easily suffocate or crush a newborn pup. You can drape a towel over half the tank to create a denlike area for your gerbils. Three inches (7.5 cm) of lit-

Multi-colored gerbils are more rare, and therefore more popular, than solid-colored gerbils.

A CRASH COURSE IN GERBIL GENETICS

Genetics is an extremely complex science. Many online resources provide an in-depth look at the genetics of gerbils. Male and female gerbils each have a gene pair of seven loci, or positioned genes, that determine the look of their offspring. These loci are A, which controls the color of the belly; C, which controls the overall level of color; D, which controls the depth of color; E, which controls the amount of gold in the fur; G, which controls the amount of gray; P, which controls eye color; and Sp, which controls spotting.

You are probably wondering what this means for your breeding pair. You know that two humans with brown hair will most likely have a child with brown hair because this color is dominant. By the same token, two gerbils with white bellies will produce offspring with white bellies because this is the dominant trait. Capital letters represent dominant genes. In gerbil genetics, AA or Aa represents a white belly. Even if a recessive gene is present in one parent gerbil, the dominant gene will overpower it. Gerbils with bellies that are the same color as their backs have aa loci. The parents of these gerbils both had the recessive gene. The only way to see the effects of the recessive gene in offspring is to pair two recessives. Be sure to consider the genetic combinations a pair of gerbils will create before you decide to breed them.

ter and a large amount of unscented tissues will provide your gerbils with the necessary materials to prepare a nest for their offspring.

Adult female gerbils go into heat about every four days. It may take some time for your gerbils to mate, especially if they are young. The best thing for a breeder to do is to give their gerbils time and space. The mating ritual of adult gerbils looks a lot like a game of tag. The male will chase the female around the tank for about two hours during the early evening hours. The female will even-

tually freeze and allow the male to mount her. Mating lasts only a few seconds, so most breeders do not witness the act. If you do happen to see your gerbils mating, you should start preparing for pups immediately. The average gerbil pregnancy lasts about twenty-five days, but it can last as long as forty-two days if the mother is still nursing another litter of pups.

From your point of view, the most important part of preparation is to start looking for good homes for the pups. Once you have lined up homes, you can focus on the needs of the mother gerbil.

Mother gerbils need little extra care during their pregnancies. The best thing you can do for the expectant gerbil is to feed her a balanced diet. Give her a little extra protein as well. Bits of scrambled egg or some cheese are just what your gerbil needs. You should also provide your mother gerbil with plenty of fresh drinking water. Pregnant gerbils do not start showing until a few days before they are ready to give birth. If possible, clean the tank before the pups are born. Once the litter arrives, any changes to the tank could stress the new parents.

Gerbils tend to give birth during the night or in the early morning hours. Mother gerbils reach between their legs and pull each pup out. The mother gerbil will eat the protein-rich placenta once all the pups are born.

Baby gerbils are born hairless and cannot see. Be sure to provide extra bedding to keep the pups and their parents warm during the first hours of life.

The entire process lasts only a few hours. Remember that male and female gerbils mate during or shortly after their pups are born, so you should expect another litter in about forty days. After birth, it is best to leave the male and female gerbils alone to tend to their pups. The mother will begin nursing the pups immediately. After about twenty-four hours, the father will take an active role in caring for the pups. He will clean them and help keep them warm.

The average number of pups in a litter is four to six. New gerbil parents often have only two or three pups in their first litter. If a single pup is born, this is a problem. One pup will not stimulate enough mother's milk and will starve. The best thing to do in that case is to foster the pup with another litter of gerbils. A mother gerbil will readily accept another pup into her clan as long as the pup is less than a week old and is not furred. A mother gerbil will see a furred pup as a threat to her litter.

FAST FACT

If a gerbil pup is stillborn or dies shortly after birth, it is best to remove it from the tank to maintain a sanitary environment for your other gerbils.

She will immediately attack and most likely kill the pup.

If your mother gerbil gives birth to a single pup, contact other breeders in your area to see if they have any young litters that can accept another pup. Fostering is usually a smooth process as long as you follow a few simple steps. First, you need to wash your hands and carefully remove the foster parents from their tank. Next, you should place the foster pup underneath the pile of baby gerbils. After allowing the pup to settle in for a few minutes, you can return the father gerbil to the tank. He will begin grooming the new pup. The mother gerbil can go back to the tank a few minutes after grooming has finished. She will find the new pup and begin nursing it.

HOW GERBILS GROW

Gerbil pups grow very quickly. The pups are born blind, deaf, and furless. For the first few weeks of life, the pups are completely dependent on their parents. You will be able to hear these tiny pink creatures squeaking for their parents throughout the day. After a few days, the skin pigment of the pups begins to indicate what color their fur will be. You can begin handling the pups when they are about a week old. It is important to wash your hands thoroughly before handling gerbil pups. Any foreign smell passed from your hands to the pups could prompt their mother to reject them. After washing your hands, spread out a pillow or a towel under the area where you will be handling the pups. Though the gerbils cannot see, they can move very quickly. They could easily slip and fall from your hands. To prevent the pups from falling, you should hold the gerbils in one hand and cover them with the other. The goal in handling newborn gerbils is to get them used to the feel and smell of human hands. After a couple of minutes, the gerbils may even settle down for a nap inside your hands. Do not keep the babies away from their parents for more than a few minutes. Gerbil parents can become nervous if their babies are away for too long. You might want to give the parent gerbils some cardboard to

FAST FACT

Some scientific studies suggest that gerbils are born with a high level of testosterone. Scientists believe that this is unpleasant for the father gerbil, who avoids the newborns for a day or two until the testosterone levels off.

nibble on as a distraction while you handle the pups.

When the pups are seven to ten days old, examine them to determine their genders. Because only female gerbils have nipples, this should be a simple process. The nipples look like tiny dents on the upper thighs, armpits, and the center of the belly. Separating your gerbils later will be much easier if you write down the distinguishing features of each male and female now. The gerbil pups will soon become so furry that it will be difficult to see these nipples. After ten days, the pups will grow thick coats of fur. At this point, they still have not opened their eyes. You should continue to handle them very carefully. Since they are much larger now, you might want to handle only one or two pups at a time. Handling the pups two or three times a week will help them become tame and friendly adult gerbils. Around the third week, the pups will open their eyes. The new sights can be very scary to gerbil pups. Even though they may seem frightened, you should continue handling them. Carefully take out one pup at a time to show it that there is nothing to fear. After a few days, the pups will become used to their new sense of sight and will calm down.

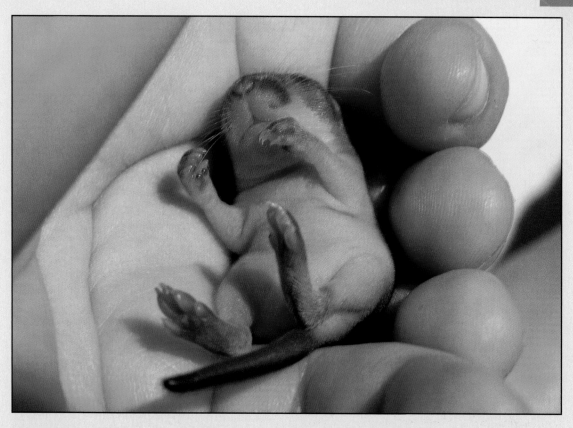

This is a Mongolian gerbil pup. Handling them early is important, but you must be sure to be very careful, as the pups are very delicate at this stage of development.

At two to three weeks, the gerbil pups will also begin eating solid foods. You can supplement regular gerbil mix with other weaning foods, such as Cheerios, shelled sunflower seeds, and plain natural yogurt. You will also want to make sure that the water bottle is low enough for the pups to get a good drink. As the pups begin to wean, the mother gerbil will begin to prepare for her next litter. You can move the pups to a nursing tank at around five weeks of age. The AGS recommends waiting until the gerbils are six weeks old before placing them in new homes.

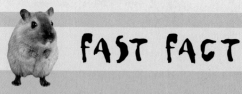

FAST FACT

Some gerbil pups may have trouble when weaning. If a pup begins losing weight, feed it kitten replacement milk from an eyedropper to give it extra nutrition.

As your gerbil pups grow, continue to handle each of them regularly, so that they become more comfortable with human interaction.

You should separate male and female pups before they reach seven weeks old to prevent them from mating.

GERBILS AND THE LAW

If you are planning to own gerbils, be sure to research and understand the laws concerning gerbils in your area. Should you decide to breed gerbils, you must also learn the laws relating to gerbils in all surrounding areas. It is illegal to own or import gerbils into the states of California and Hawaii, for example. Lawmakers in these states worry that gerbils may be released into the wild, which could potentially wreak havoc on the states' ecosystems. They worry that gerbils would reproduce quickly and destroy crops. Certain counties or municipalities might also have local laws about keeping gerbils.

As a gerbil breeder, you have an obligation not to knowingly allow anyone living in one of these restricted areas to purchase or adopt your gerbils. If you do give a gerbil to someone living in an area that has restrictions on gerbils, you could face legal action. Worst of all, illegal gerbils might be euthanized if proper homes in other states cannot be found.

SHOWING GERBILS

Showing your gerbils can be a fun and easy way to meet other people who share your enthusiasm for these special creatures. The AGS usually has two shows each year—one in the Northeast and another in the Midwest. Gerbil shows provide breeders with the latest information about gerbil care. Attending shows is also a good way to learn about breed standards. Gerbil societies develop standards that judges use to evaluate gerbils. These standards usually deal with coloration and temperament. Gerbils that excel in their groupings receive ribbons and awards. Your gerbils will also get the opportunity to participate in enjoyable activities, such as races and talent shows. Gerbil shows are also a lot of fun for young children. This is a great way to introduce children to the many different kinds of gerbils.

Remember that breeding and caring for gerbils is a big responsibility. Breeding is a commitment, not a casual undertaking. Gerbils need a lot of attention to grow into friendly pets. If you have a lot of love and patience, you might find breeding and showing your gerbils to be a fulfilling and rewarding experience.

CHAPTER FOUR

The Best Possible Beginning

Before bringing gerbils home, you should prepare their new residence. Even before buying your pets, you will need to buy supplies, housing, and food. Chapter 5 will tell you what food to buy for your gerbils. Moving to a new home is stressful for gerbils, so you should try to make it as comfortable for them as possible. If you have already established a safe, appropriate habitat for them, they can get settled as soon as possible.

A GERBIL'S HOME

The most expensive piece of gerbil equipment is the cage or tank. You

---

Before bringing gerbils into your home, make sure that you have prepared an appropriate habitat that includes safe chew toys and places for them to hide and play.

can get suitable gerbil housing at a local pet store, on the Internet, or through the classified ads in your local newspaper. With all the available choices, choosing a gerbil cage may seem overwhelming, but some general rules will help you decide what is best for your gerbils.

The size of your gerbils' new home is very important. You should buy the largest gerbil cage you can afford and have space for. Gerbils are active, so they need a lot of room to tunnel, play, and exercise. If your gerbils' cage is too small, they will become irritable and fight. A small, cramped cage becomes dirty, smelly, and difficult to clean. Your gerbils' health and happiness will increase in direct proportion to the size of their cage. If they have more room to play and explore, they will be better pets. In the wild, gerbils are very neat, organized animals. They often have separate areas for eating, sleeping, and going to the bathroom. You should provide a large enough cage for them to have separate areas for all these activities. Your gerbils will also need one or two exercise wheels to ensure that they get enough exercise.

Cages come in many varieties, so keep gerbils' traits in mind. Although gerbils sometimes climb in the wild, they are natural ground dwellers. They enjoy climbing up things but often have trouble climbing back down, so high spaces could be dangerous for your gerbils. Gerbils also prefer a lot of floor space in which to run around. Some manufacturers develop gerbil cages that are two or three stories tall with minimal floor space. Gerbils adapt easily, so they

Gerbils will thrive in an enclosure with an area of about 10 gallons (38 liters). Wood chips or plastic tunnels will help your pet to feel at home.

will get used to these tall, narrow cages. These cages, however, are poor homes for gerbils. You should choose a single-story cage with a large floor area, rather than a tall, narrow cage. The more space your Gerbil has, the easier it will be for him to get the proper amount of exercise. This will help prevent your gerbil from becoming overweight.

Gerbils are notorious for trying to escape from their cages. This is not because they do not like their homes—they just like to explore. As a result, you will have to keep certain precautions in mind when you are choosing your gerbils' home. You should be able to reach into your gerbils' cage for cleaning, feeding, and handling. If your gerbils' cage or tank is too deep, providing fresh food and water, and cleaning the cage, will be more difficult. Cages come with their latches and doors in many different places. It is best to choose one with a large front door, a latching top, or both, and you should be able to fit your hand into the cage easily to get your gerbils. Remember, however, that you do not want your gerbils to be able to push the door or latch open. The cage needs to be very secure to prevent gerbil escapes.

INTRODUCING TWO OLDER GERBILS

While young gerbils that are six to eight weeks old are easy to introduce to each other, older gerbils need careful observation and handling when they are being introduced. There is, however, a method for introducing two older gerbils.

Start by placing a wire-mesh divider between the two halves of a small cage or aquarium. The wire-mesh divider should fit snugly to keep your gerbils from sneaking through. Put each gerbil on a different side of the divider. Make sure each gerbil has its own nest box, bedding, food, and water. A few times each day, switch the gerbils, placing each into the space on the opposite side of the divider. This will blend your gerbils' scents, and your gerbils will eventually share one common scent.

After about a week, put both gerbils into an area outside their cage where you can keep an eye on them. Let them sniff and play, but if they fight, you should separate them immediately. You will have to repeat the switching process until the gerbils are ready to get along. Once your gerbils are prepared to be friends, you can put them both into their regular, large tank or cage with some of the bedding from their smaller aquarium.

CHOOSING THE RIGHT CAGE

Before choosing your gerbils' new home, you will have to decide whether to buy a glass aquarium, a wire-frame cage, or some other type of cage, such as a combination wire and plastic cage.

GLASS AQUARIUMS: A ten-gallon (38 liter) glass aquarium, often sold in the fish or reptile section of a pet store, is a good home for two gerbils, as long as it has the proper screen. These glass aquariums are sometimes sold with secure, wire-screen covers and latches. These covers and latches are essential to making the glass aquarium a good home for your gerbils. Gerbils are clever and can escape easily, so these aquariums always need to stay covered. The latches are necessary to keep your gerbils from pushing the screen to the side and sneaking out. If you are still afraid that your gerbils might

FAST FACT

If your gerbil has any wood toys, they should not be washed in water, as this could cause them to splinter. You can scrape or file any wood toys and the metal bars of a wire-frame cage.

FAST FACT

Although it is uncommon, gerbils that have been happily living together can sometimes start to fight unexpectedly. If this behavior persists, you will have to separate the former friends.

escape, you could put extra weight, such as books or stones, on top of the screen. You can also see if your local pet store sells extra latches, which are probably safer and more secure. The screen should come off easily so you can reach your gerbils and all parts of their cage.

Some manufacturers make aquarium toppers that are different from the simple wire-screen covers. These toppers add a second—or even third—story to your gerbils' aquarium, which makes for a section of their tank that has better ventilation and extra floor space. Remember, however, that your gerbils are not the best climbers in the rodent kingdom. If you opt for one of these tank toppers, you should provide ways for your gerbils to climb into and down from the second and third stories easily without injuring themselves.

Gerbils like to dig and tunnel, which means that they will kick their bedding and food outside of their tanks. This will make quite a mess around a wire-frame cage. If you use a glass aquarium, however, the sides are closed in, which will prevent the mess from spreading to your home. This will also prevent a draft from affecting your gerbils' health because of the enclosed sides.

If you do not keep the glass aquarium clean, however, it will become very dirty, making the glass difficult to see through. Glass aquariums do not provide good ventilation because they are enclosed. If you are not diligent about cleaning your gerbils' home, ammonia gas from their urine can build up. If you do not regularly clean your gerbils' home, this ammonia buildup can make your gerbils sick. The ammonia will damage your gerbils' respiratory systems, which could be fatal.

WIRE-FRAME CAGES: If you decide to provide your gerbils with a wire-frame cage as a home, the cage should be at least twenty inches (51 cm) long, twelve inches (30.5 cm) wide, and ten inches (25.5 cm) deep. This will be enough space for your two gerbils. Wire-frame cages, often made of galvanized steel, provide more ventilation than glass aquariums do, and you can still see your pets through the side of their tank, just as you can with a glass aquarium. Most wire-frame cages come equipped with a metal or plastic slide-out or snap-off bottom tray that makes cleaning easy, and the plastic bottoms often come in stylish colors. You should make sure, however, that the cage's wire bottom keeps your gerbils away from the plastic tray; if your gerbils can reach that tray, they will chew and damage it.

The wire-frame cage needs to have a large front or top door to allow you to reach inside the cage to feed, clean, and handle your gerbils. Some wire-frame cages are made with a large door and a removable side to make cleaning inside the cage easier. The door latches will have to be secure so that your gerbils cannot escape easily by pushing the door out. Make sure that any wire-frame cage you decide on does not have sharp, metal corners and edges that could injure your gerbils.

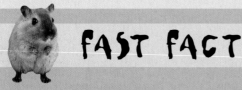

FAST FACT

If you ever notice broken, damaged, or chewed parts in your gerbils' cage or tank, you must replace these parts immediately. Gerbils are very clever, and it will not take them long to figure out an escape route.

Wire-frame cages with plastic bottoms can make a good home for your gerbils. However, these cages have several drawbacks. Your gerbils will probably chew on the cage bars, which can be annoying. Bits of their bedding or floor covering will be constantly pushed out of the cage when they are active. Also, because these cages are open, your gerbils may become sick if their home is placed in a drafty area.

The wire mesh and bars of the cage should be very sturdy, not flimsy. Be sure to read the information and labeling of the wire-frame cage you are thinking about buying. A cage for hamsters or mice may not be large enough to house your gerbils. The bars should not be more than one-half inch (13 mm) apart—you do not want your gerbils to squeeze through the bars of their home. If you purchase a wire-frame cage made for larger animals such as rabbits or guinea pigs, the bars will probably be more than one-half inch (13 mm) apart. In that case, you will have to cover the cage with heavy gauge wire meshing, which you can buy at a local hardware store. You should attach this mesh using strong metal clips, not plastic ties, thin wire, or string—your gerbils can chew through these materials. Fasten the mesh securely and tightly to the wire-frame cage to prevent your gerbils from squeezing between the two layers in an escape attempt. This could trap or injure them.

If you decide on a wire-frame cage, remember that it provides good ventilation, which also means that it could be drafty. You will have to make sure that you do not put the wire-frame cage in a drafty spot in front of a window or door. Your gerbils' urine can also weaken the metal in the cage bottom and tray, damaging the cage. You will have to clean your gerbils' bathroom area frequently, and you should line the bottom of the tray with newspaper. Your gerbils should not be able to get to this newspaper. If they chew the paper, it could make them sick.

You will also have to make sure the bottom of the wire-frame cage is safe for your gerbils. If the cage has a wire floor at the bottom, your gerbils' small feet could become tangled in the wire. This is not a problem in cages with solid bottoms. In a cage with a wire floor, you will have to put a thick layer of bedding at the bottom to protect your gerbils from getting their feet caught (and to prevent their waste from landing on the floor).

You should try to choose a wire-frame cage with high sides on the bottom tray. Your gerbils will kick their bedding out of the cage while digging, which will make a mess around their cage. Putting several layers of newspaper outside and around your gerbils' cage can keep this from getting out of control. You might also choose to put your gerbils' cage in a large kitty litter pan to catch anything that they kick out. A cloth seed guard (available at pet stores) under the cage will also help keep your floor clean.

OTHER GERBIL HOMES

Some gerbil cages are a combination of wire screen and plastic. These cages look fun and exciting because they provide your gerbils with various plastic tubes and enclosures—they look more like playgrounds than houses. You should avoid these cages, however, because they provide very little ventilation for your gerbils. If each little section is not cleaned frequently, the tubes and small spaces can become dirty and smelly. The plastic tubes are easy for your gerbils to chew through, too, affording them simple escape routes. Your

Cages like this one look like fun, but be aware that the plastic tubes are difficult to clean.

gerbils' nails can also scratch the plastic, making it difficult to see your gerbils through the clear tubes. Many manufacturers have tried to improve the design of these combination cages, so if you do decide you want one, find one with the best available ventilation. You should also check that the doors and latches are secure and large enough for you to reach into the cage.

Some gerbils are escape artists, and certain cages are not suitable for your gerbils. Your gerbils' home needs to be a well-constructed, escape-proof enclosure. A wooden cage is not suitable for gerbils. Gerbils have strong, sharp teeth and their jaws and muscles are extremely powerful. They can easily chew through a wooden cage. Wood also absorbs urine and odors, so wooden habitats are unsanitary and difficult to clean.

WHERE TO PUT A GERBIL'S HOME

To find an ideal place to put your gerbils' home, you should consider where you spend the most time in your home. Your gerbils will be a part of your family, so you do not want to put them in a room with few visitors, where your gerbils may feel isolated. You will want to watch your gerbils and enjoy them as pets. You should not put your gerbils on the floor or on a high shelf. The temperature near the floor is often much lower than it is in the rest of the house, and a high shelf may be warmer. It will also be difficult to watch your gerbils if their cage is very high or very low.

The best place to put your gerbils is on an eye-level table or dresser. At first, movement in the room may cause your gerbils to become nervous and hide under their bedding or in their nest box (see "Your Gerbils' Supplies" later in this chapter), but your gerbils will get used to the movement and noise in the room. Your gerbils' home should be in a place where you will see them every day so they will not get lonely or feel neglected.

You should not expose your gerbils to a draft, or place their cage where the temperature varies greatly. That means the cage should not be put in front of a heating vent, an air-conditioner, a window, or a door. Make sure your gerbils are not in direct sunlight, as this could cause variations in the temperature. You should try to keep your gerbils in a dry environment with a temperature between sixty and seventy degrees Fahrenheit (15.5–21 degrees Celsius) and a relative humidity between 30 and 50 percent. Humidity greater than 50 percent can cause gerbils a lot of stress, making their fur stand out and appear matted. Absorbent bedding material can help keep the cage's humidity under control, but it is still necessary to continually monitor your gerbils for signs of distress if you live in a humid environment.

If you put your gerbils' cage in a place where they get very cold, they may become overweight or lazy, and they may even try to hibernate. Never keep your gerbils in a basement or a garage. Automobile exhaust, moisture, dampness, and temperature variation can cause your gerbils to become sick or even die.

You should also make sure your gerbils are not in the line of sight of larger pets like cats and dogs. If you have cats or dogs, they might constantly sniff and stare at your gerbils, which could stress your gerbils.

Gerbils are sensitive to ultrasonic noises—sound frequencies that are too high for humans to hear. Computers, televisions, and other electronic devices produce ultrasonic sounds, so avoid putting your pet gerbils on top of or near electronics. In general, gerbils will prefer quiet places in your home.

Remember that anything you place near your gerbils' home is in danger of being chewed and destroyed. Gerbils will try to pull nearby papers and fabrics (think curtains or drapes) into the cage if they can.

BEDDING MATERIALS

At the bottom of your gerbils' home, you will need to place bedding materials. Bedding will absorb moisture from water bottle leaks and urine. This is important to keeping your gerbils' habitat a warm, dry environment, which will maintain your gerbils' health. In addition, the bedding materials will reduce the odor

of your gerbils, their urine, and their waste. Your gerbils will also tunnel in the bedding materials—one of their favorite pastimes.

Pet stores carry many different kinds of bedding materials. You can provide your gerbils with untreated wood shavings such as pine and aspen. You should never give your gerbils cedar wood shavings, however, because some experts believe they may cause health problems for

Keep your gerbils far away from other pets, like cats and dogs. They may think your pet is a toy or a snack.

The bedding in your gerbils' cage should be replaced each time you clean the enclosure. Many veterinarians believe aspen shavings make the nicest bedding for gerbils.

gerbils. Although this is controversial, it is best to be on the safe side and avoid cedar. You can also purchase bedding made from recycled paper or wood pulp. These bedding materials are a little more expensive, but they are made to control odor. Recycled paper bedding does not contain heavy metals, dyes, or inks, which may be toxic to gerbils.

No matter what bedding you provide, you should cover the bottom four inches (10 cm) of the tank or cage with it. This will allow your gerbils to burrow. You should try to get dust-free bedding because dust can cause respiratory problems for your gerbil. Wood pulp and recycled paper bedding usually has less dust than wood shavings do.

THE PROPER SUPPLIES

FOOD DISH: Once your gerbils' home is established, it is time to pick up supplies for them. You need to consider how you will give your gerbils their food. If you chose a wire-frame cage, you can get a food dish that attaches to the side to prevent your gerbils from tipping it over. If you get a dish that stands on its own, make sure you get one that is too heavy for your gerbils to tip over. A large ceramic dish will be too heavy for your gerbils to move. It may seem like your gerbils do not need a dish because they carry their food off to eat it. Some gerbil owners, in fact, feed their gerbils simply by scattering food on the cage floor. However, you might prefer to give your gerbils a food dish to monitor how much they are eating, and to keep the food from being contaminated by urine and waste. If you keep your gerbils' home extremely clean, you can spread some food around to encourage exercise and foraging. Chapter 5 will discuss the types of food that are best for your gerbils.

Your gerbil's water bottle should always be filled with fresh, clean water.

WATER BOTTLE: As creatures that are native to the desert, gerbils do not need to drink a lot of water. However, you should provide them with at least six to eight fluid ounces of fresh water each day. The best way to do this is to buy a hamster-sized, gravity-fed water bottle. These water bottles attach to the side of your gerbils' tank or cage. If you put water in a dish, your gerbils will knock it over. Make sure the water bottle's tip is easy for your gerbils to reach. It should not be so high that they have to stretch for it, or so low that it touches their bedding. If the water bottle's end is touching anything, it will leak. This could make a big mess—especially if the water bottle is over the food dish or the nest box. Be sure to empty and refill the bottle daily to ensure that their water remains fresh and clean.

NEST BOX: Your gerbils need a nest box. A nest box is like a bedroom that provides security while your gerbils are sleeping. It also gives your gerbils a place to hide. You can buy a pre-made nest box at a pet store. Some are chewable, while others are made of hard plastic or ceramic. You can also make your own nest box out of a cardboard box or a milk carton. If your gerbils have a chewable nest box, you will need to replace it when it gets destroyed.

You should also give your gerbils nesting materials. Tissue paper or paper towels are good nesting material. Your gerbils will shred the paper and make a nest. Pet stores sell nesting materials, but you should never buy synthetic fiber bedding. Your gerbils' feet can get tangled in these fibers, leading to injury. They may also eat the nesting material, which they may not be able to pass, causing a gastrointestinal obstruction. Nesting materials that are compressed, made from cotton, or sold for hamsters, are all acceptable for your gerbils.

DUST BATH AND MORE: You will need to provide your gerbils with a dust bath for grooming purposes. Chapter 5 will explain how to set up a dust bath. In addition, your gerbils will need toys and one or two exercise wheels. Chapter 7 will tell you the best toys and exercise wheels for your gerbils. It will also delve into how to make your own toys for your gerbils.

CLEANING THE CAGE

Ammonia from your gerbils' urine will build up and cause an unpleasant odor in their tank. This will make owning gerbils less pleasant for you, and if you do not clean your gerbils' home regularly, it can make your gerbils sick. Although some bedding is designed to reduce odor and moisture, you will still need to keep your gerbils' home clean. How often you clean your gerbils' tank depends on the size of their home. If you keep your gerbils in a relatively large tank, you should clean it once every two weeks. If you keep your gerbils in a smaller tank, you should clean it once a week. You should try to clean your gerbils' home before it smells. Place your gerbils in a secure carrier or travel box while you are cleaning their cage.

To clean your gerbils' home, you will need to remove old bedding and replace it with fresh, clean, dry bedding. Between cleanings, you can partially change the bedding. Gerbils will establish a bathroom area in their cage, so you may have to change this bedding between cleanings. You can also provide your gerbils with a small, plastic litter pan. You can buy a small litter pan made for rabbits or ferrets at the pet store or online. You may have to do some experimenting to figure out what will persuade your gerbils to use the litter pan. Try placing it above the bedding and under the bedding. You should put their familiar bedding material in the litter pan. Unfortunately, your gerbils will not always use this litter pan; they may simply chew the plastic and destroy it.

During your regular tank cleanings, you will have to replace your gerbils' nesting materials in the nest box. Wash anything that is plastic or ceramic, such as their food dish, their toys, and possibly their nest box. You should replace anything

FAST FACT

While you are cleaning your gerbils' home, you can place them and their nest box in the bathtub. The slippery sides of the bathtub will prevent them from escaping, but you should still make sure to close the bathroom door!

made of cardboard that is chewed or smelly.

Gerbils do not like clean cages. They work hard to make everything smell like them, so after a cleaning, your gerbils will be busy rubbing their scent onto everything. If you do

GERBIL CARRIERS

Your gerbils will need a carrier that serves as a temporary home or travel box. This carrier is useful while you are cleaning your gerbils' home, to travel to veterinarian appointments, and for other traveling. Your gerbils' carrier can be any small, secure tank or cage. You should not put your gerbils into cardboard carriers, however, because your gerbils can easily chew through these—especially on long trips.

Some companies make rectangular, plastic enclosures with snap-on lids—often called small animal habitats. Unless these enclosures are at least the same size as a ten-gallon (40 l) aquarium, they are not large enough to house a pair of gerbils, so they are inadequate as permanent homes. You can use these enclosures, however, to transport your gerbils to your home or to the veterinarian. They also provide a safe space for your gerbils while you clean their permanent home. Keep in mind that these small animal habitats break easily, so be careful with them.

partial cleanings and leave some toys, your gerbils will be happy to smell something familiar. Once a month, however, you should wash their cage or tank by scrubbing it very thoroughly with hot, soapy water. If you need to, you can disinfect the cage or tank with bleach. You should do this by diluting no more than one tablespoon (15 ml) of bleach in a gallon (4 l) of cold water. For an especially thorough cleaning, you could immerse the cage or tank in a bathtub for at least thirty seconds in this solution. Then rinse the cage thoroughly with a clean, wet washcloth and let it air dry. It needs to air dry so the bleach can evaporate. Simply drying it with a towel will expose your gerbils to harmful bleach. During this thorough cleaning, you need to wash the water bottle, food dish, toys, and nesting box.

IF YOUR GERBILS ESCAPE

Despite all your hard work to prevent your gerbils from escaping, one or both of your gerbils could still manage to escape from their cage. Your gerbils could even run away while you are playing with them. An escape is dangerous for your gerbils. They will not have access to food and

Monthly cleaning of your gerbils' cage is vital to maintaining their health. Be sure that their cage is wiped clean of all cleaning products before reintroducing your gerbils, as the chemicals can make your pets sick.

water, so they are in danger of becoming dehydrated or starving. If you have other pets, such as cats or dogs, your gerbil may look like a home invader or a fun toy, which puts it in danger of being eaten or injured. Your gerbils may even destroy your home by chewing on your furniture or your walls, or they could injure themselves by chewing on electrical wires. If your gerbil gets outside, the chances that you will find it are not good.

The best thing to do is to assume that your gerbil or gerbils are still in the house. The first step is to conduct a thorough search of your house. If you think you know which room your gerbil is in, you should check that room first, closing off any exits to the room before you begin searching. Then search one room at a time. Once you have searched a room, close the door, and place a towel or books under the door and in cracks to make sure the gerbil cannot enter that room. This will narrow the areas you have to search. While you are searching your home, keep on hand your gerbils' nest box

If one of your gerbils escapes, don't panic. Shut all doors and block as many possible exits as you can to prevent your friend from getting outside. Taking a methodical approach will increase your chances of finding him.

and some treats, such as sunflower seeds.

Remember that you could startle your gerbil if you make any sudden moves or loud noises. So if you see the gerbil, move slowly and speak quietly. Try to get close to your gerbil, and offer it some treats. You can also put down the nest box and leave a trail of treats to it. If none of these ploys work, you should put your gerbils' home on the floor in the room where you think it is loose. If only one gerbil is loose, do not leave the cage door open; if you do, the gerbil that did not get loose will leave the cage to join your other gerbil. Instead, leave a trail of treats to the cage, and put your gerbils' nest box next to the cage. If you do this, you should provide the gerbil still in the cage with a new nest box. Your loose gerbil may come to sleep and eat in its old nest box.

If your gerbil refuses to return to its home, it may be hoarding the sunflower seeds and taking them to its new, secret home. You will have to trap your gerbil in this situation. You can purchase harmless traps from a local hardware store or pet store and bait them with peanut butter or oats. You should use the traps made for mice—not rats—and use more than one trap.

GERBIL-PROOFING YOUR HOUSE

Some common things in your house may be hazards for gerbils. Be careful not to put your gerbils in danger by placing them near hazards. If you let your gerbils out to play, you should make sure they are not near hazards. If your gerbil escapes, you will have to act quickly to gerbil-proof your house. One common hazard for gerbils is other pets, such as dogs and cats. Even if your other

Cables and cords can be a hazard to your gerbils.

pets are friendly, their instincts may tell them that gerbils are toys or food. If you take your gerbils out of their cage, make sure your other pets cannot get to them.

Electrical wires and appliances are another gerbil hazard. Gerbils, because they make their own ultrasonic sounds, are sensitive to the ultrasonic sounds of electrical appliances. Electrical wires are a hazard to gerbils because they love to chew. They will chew on electrical wires and cords if they can get to them. You should always place your electrical wires securely behind a protective strip to protect your gerbils. This is especially important if your gerbils escape.

When your gerbils are outside their cage, make sure they cannot get to any houseplants. Some houseplants are poisonous to gerbils. You should also take precautions so your gerbils cannot chew on anything with dangerous and

harmful chemicals. Remember that your gerbils are much smaller than other pets are, so if they ingest even a small amount of chemicals, it could be fatal for them.

Another hazard to gerbils is their own diminutive size. When your gerbils are out of their cage, do not move furniture or open doors without looking. Make sure no one sits or steps on your gerbil. Try to keep your gerbils from getting on anything high that they could fall from—any fall could kill your gerbil. You should also close all doors and windows. If your gerbils get outside, you are not likely to find them again, and they will be in constant danger.

When you take your gerbils out of their cage, place them in an area with rough floors or carpets. Smooth floors can sometimes make it difficult for gerbils to run and stop.

Avoiding these gerbil hazards is an important part of being a responsible gerbil owner.

CHAPTER FIVE

Nutrition, Exercise, Grooming, and Training

In the wild, gerbils eat plants, fruits, grains, nuts, and a lot of seeds. They are omnivores—they eat mostly plants, but they also enjoy the occasional tasty bug. Pet stores sell gerbil foods that try to mimic this diet as closely as possible. Pet gerbils should have access to a healthy, varied diet. Aside from the vitamins and minerals in packaged foods, gerbils enjoy fresh food and some occasional treats so that they get a healthy amount of vitamins and protein.

PACKAGED FOODS: Most packaged gerbil foods are available at well-stocked pet stores and provide gerbils

Fruits are a necesssary part of a balanced gerbil diet, but should be given in moderation.

with the right balance of nutrients. Many experts suggest that packaged foods should consist mostly of oats. The food should include as little corn as possible, because corn is mostly filler. Try to find a gerbil food that includes animal protein. Protein helps your gerbil maintain muscle and fight sickness. You have to remember, however, that foods with animal protein spoil faster than other types of packaged foods. Pay attention to any use-by or sell-by dates marked on the bag, and keep open packages in a sealed container, preferably in a dark space. Proper storage will keep the food fresh.

FRESH FOODS: Gerbils can get extra protein from many different sources. Try feeding your gerbils a little bit of dry cat food, a chopped up hard-boiled egg, or even a live insect. Introduce new foods slowly, so your gerbils can get used to them. Start with a small amount of a new food to see how you gerbils like it, as well as how their bodies deal with the new nutrients.

FRUITS, VEGETABLES, AND HAY: Gerbils enjoy a variety of fresh foods. Gerbils get all sorts of important nutrients from fruits and vegetables. The water they get from produce also helps keep them

hydrated. Gerbils like many different fruits and vegetables, such as sliced apples, bananas, broccoli, carrots, chicory, corn, cucumbers, endive, peas, and cooked potatoes. You should make sure that a majority of your gerbils' diet is not fruits and vegetables; too much will result in diarrhea.

If you feed your gerbils fresh food, you should check their tank a few hours later. You have to remove from the tank any perishable food that has not been consumed. The old food could begin to smell, or if your gerbils do decide to eat the old food, they may become ill. When giving gerbils fresh food, also remember to wash all food thoroughly. Many fruits and vegetables are treated with pesticides that can cause sickness. Gerbils are especially sensitive to these chemicals because they are so small.

Gerbils also enjoy a little hay sometimes. Hay is good for the

FAST FACT

A good premixed food for gerbils will have about 12 percent protein content and between 6 and 8 percent fat content. You should never give your gerbils food with more than 10 percent fat content!

gerbil's digestive system, and gerbils enjoy chewing it. Most pet stores sell small amounts of hay. If you are not sure you are buying the right stuff, ask the employees if the hay on sale is safe for gerbils.

TREATS: Just like humans, gerbils enjoy special treats. Some tasty treats for gerbils are mealworms, chopped hard-boiled eggs, and plain natural yogurt. Sunflower seeds, pumpkin seeds, and unsalted natural peanuts are all tasty treats for gerbils as well. Remember that all these items are treats and should not make up too much of your gerbils' diets. You should never give too many treats to your gerbils. Nuts and seeds are high in fat, and gerbils can get sick if they eat too many. Sunflower seeds seem to be a big favorite of gerbils, but the seeds are low in calcium and can upset your gerbils' balance of nutrients. They can also result in obesity because of their high fat content.

Experts are always suggesting new treats to give to gerbils, so if your pets like to try new things, keep up on your gerbil treat research. Healthy dog biscuits and dry bread are nice treats because they provide carbohydrates as well as something solid to chew. Gerbils enjoy pieces of crackers, Cheerios, and puffed rice cereals. Sugary cereals, however, are very unhealthy for gerbils.

INSECTS: You do not have to feed your gerbils insects, but some gerbils really enjoy this protein-rich treat. Many pet shops sell live insects as feed for pets. Although many experts recommend feeding gerbils meal-

Your gerbil will appreciate an occasional snack. However, only give him food that is good for him. Avoid cookies and other human snacks, as they can upset his digestive system.

Never feed your gerbils chocolate, candy, or junk food.

worms, crickets also make a yummy snack. Gerbils enjoy chasing the creatures around the cage before eating them, and gerbils get more calcium from eating crickets than they get from eating mealworms.

FOODS TO AVOID: Do not give gerbils sorrel, raw beans, or moldy potatoes. Green potatoes are also unsafe. Although many gerbil owners suggest giving gerbils lettuce, some experts warn that lettuce and cabbage are not good for your gerbils and may cause diarrhea.

HOW AND WHEN TO FEED GERBILS: When you feed your gerbils, you should always put some food into a food dish. The food dish needs to be large and ceramic so the gerbils cannot tip it over. You can also spread the food around the cage or sprinkle it in a small pile. No matter how you serve it, gerbils will probably spread their food all over the cage. Gerbils like to forage for their food. They also like to bury their

food in their bedding so that other gerbils cannot get to it.

Gerbils do not usually overeat, so do not worry about overfeeding your gerbil. Follow the recommended serving size listed on the bag of food and feed you gerbils every day. A good rule is to serve one tablespoon (15 ml) of food for each gerbil, but make sure they are eating all the food—not just picking our their favorite parts and hoping for a new batch to arrive. If they do pick and choose, do not refill the food until they finish the whole batch.

If they eat their food very quickly, feel free to give them a little more. Just like humans, all gerbils have different appetites. If you have more than two gerbils, make sure all the gerbils are getting their fair share. You might have to do a little rearranging so that each gerbil gets a share of the food.

Vitamins and minerals, such as calcium, phosphorus, and sodium, are necessary for your gerbils' health. If you feed your gerbils a balanced, varied diet, supplements are probably not necessary, unless your veterinarian recommends them.

COPROPHAGY: Your gerbils get some valuable nutrients from their fellow gerbils, but chances are that you will not see this happening since they usually do it late at night or early in the morning.

Some nutrients are processed in a gerbil's digestive system. Although some of those nutrients are absorbed by the body, gerbils cannot get all their nutrients in this way. They get the remainder by eating droppings directly from the anus of fellow gerbils. This process is called coprophagy, and it allows gerbils to get very important vitamins that they need to live happy, healthy lives.

WATER

Your gerbils need a water source in their home, and the best type of water source is a hamster-sized gravity-fed bottle that attaches to the cage or that goes over the top of the tank. A water bowl is not suitable for gerbils. The water will spill and soil the bedding, making life uncomfortable for the gerbils and possibly making them sick. Proper bottles are sold in just about every pet store.

Be sure to remove the water bottle once a day and fill it with fresh water. Once a week, you should clean the water bottle thoroughly. You should also check the bottle daily to ensure that it is dispensing water properly. Water should drip from these bottles only when gerbils come for a drink; otherwise, the water could drip out slowly and saturate the bedding. Remove any wet bedding from the tank immediately. You should replace a leaking water bottle promptly.

GROOMING YOUR GERBILS

Gerbils are naturally clean animals that spend many waking hours grooming themselves. They use their tiny hands to wash their faces, and they use their hind legs to clean their ears. Your gerbils will also groom each other. Gerbils' companions will often help by cleaning hard-to-reach places, like the neck and back. If you notice that your gerbil looks unkempt, you should quickly check its health. Sick gerbils often do not have the energy to maintain their normal grooming routines.

Although gerbils do not need too much of your help to stay clean, grooming is a good way to bond with your gerbils. Grooming is also a great time to monitor your gerbils' physical condition. While you are grooming your gerbils, you can check their eyes, nose, and ears to make sure that they are free of discharge. You can also examine each of their bodies to see that they do not have lumps or bumps and that their skin is not flaky

GERBIL PARASITES

Just like other pets, gerbils can get parasites, such as mites and fleas. Keeping your gerbils and their home clean will help prevent fleas. The most common source of infestation is other pets, such as dogs or cats that go outside.

If your gerbils become infested with parasites, you may observe the same symptoms that you would see in larger animals. For example, your gerbils may scratch themselves repeatedly, or you might see dark flakes of flea droppings on their skin or fur.

If fleas or mites do infest your pets, ask your veterinarian what treatment is appropriate for gerbils. Usually, the vet will recommend an ointment or shampoo that can be used on young kittens. You'll also have to treat your entire house, as well as your other pets, to eliminate the parasites completely.

or dry. You should also look carefully at their fur. Each gerbil's coat should look shiny and smooth. A gerbil's coat should not have any dry, bald spots. If you notice any sticky patches of fur, clean the fur gently with a damp cloth. You should dry the area immediately to keep your gerbil from catching a chill.

GROOMING SUPPLIES: Although gerbils do not require many supplies to stay clean, you should keep some items on hand at all times. Some pet stores sell sprays and wipes for small animals such as gerbils, but these are not necessary for your gerbils. If you wash your gerbils, they could get sick. A wet gerbil could get a chill in cold weather very easily. It is best to avoid these products. The grooming supplies you should keep on hand for your gerbils include chinchilla sand (available in most pet stores), cotton swabs, small safety scissors, a pair of small nail clippers, and a small kitten brush.

DUST BATHS: While taking a dust bath might not seem like a good way to get clean, rolling around in chinchilla sand actually removes parasites from your gerbils' fur. Dust baths can also be very entertaining for both you and your gerbils. To prepare a dust bath, place chinchilla sand in a container that is deep enough to hold about a half-inch (13 mm) of dust. You should also make sure it is large enough to allow your gerbils to roll and flip over. A dust bath once a week will keep your gerbils happy. You should remove the container from the cage or tank when they're done with their bath, and replace the sand after two or three baths.

NAIL CARE: Gerbils will usually chew their tiny nails to keep them short. If you notice that your gerbils' nails are getting a little long, you can ask your veterinarian to show you how to trim them. Gerbils are very small, so trimming their nails is difficult and dangerous. You should use small nail clippers, and you should ask another person to help you. This will allow you to clip the nails while your helper gently restrains the gerbil.

EAR CARE: Gerbils do not need help cleaning their ears. If you notice your gerbils scratching their ears more than usual, they may have ear mites. It is important to take your gerbils to the veterinarian for ear mite treatment. Your veterinarian will prescribe a medication that you must carefully administer over several weeks.

BRUSHING: While you do not need to brush your gerbils to keep them clean, brushing your gerbils is a great way to bond with them. You can use a small-bristle kitten brush, purchased from a pet store, or even a soft-bristle toothbrush. Not all gerbils like to be brushed, so you should start by gently stroking each gerbil's fur with the brush to see how it responds. If your gerbil stays still, it probably enjoys being brushed. If it runs away from the brush, it would probably rather be left alone. With a

It's quite difficult to trim your gerbil's nails. Using small clippers, snip off the end of the nail close to the tip. If you cut too deep, you will nick the blood supply to the nail, called the quick. This will hurt your gerbil and cause his nail to bleed. You can stop the bleeding with a little cornstarch or a styptic pencil.

It can be fun for everyone to let your gerbils explore your home. Just be sure to keep a close eye on them so that they do not get themselves into trouble.

little regular grooming, you can help keep your gerbils looking and feeling their best.

GERBILS ON THE MOVE

Your gerbils need a lot of exercise, so make sure to provide them with everything they need to get it. Chapter 7 will discuss toys for your gerbils' cage. Gerbils also need some exercise out of their cage in a gerbil-proof room.

Running around outside their cage is very good for gerbils. Just like people, gerbils need exercise to stay healthy. Being outside the cage allows gerbils to get physical exercise, and it allows them to get mental exercise. While your gerbils are out of their cage, they can see, smell, and explore new things. Gerbils enjoy this chance to broaden their horizons. You should make sure you know the correct way to handle your gerbils before taking them out of their cage.

When your gerbils are finished playing, you want them to get safely back to their cages, but you should not pick them up and carry them to their tank. Instead, give your gerbils a way to get back to their tank on their own. They might just go right back to their cage when they get hungry. If your gerbils do not seem to want to go back to their cage, you should hold a paper towel roll at a place where the gerbils can crawl inside. Once they crawl inside, carefully carry the paper towel roll back to the tank, and set it in the cage. The gerbils will come out when they are ready.

Take all the proper precautions so your gerbils do not get injured during their ventures outside their cage. Look out for baskets and boxes that gerbils can get into, but will not be able to get out of. Most houseplants are toxic to gerbils, so don't allow your pets the chance to nibble on them. Watch also for any other dangerous materials that gerbils might want to chew on—and remember that gerbils like to chew on everything!

TAMING AND HANDLING YOUR GERBIL

Make sure your gerbils are calm before you start handling them. Give gerbils a few days to settle into their new home before attempting to hold them. Remember that no one likes to be awakened from a sound sleep, so make sure your gerbils are awake before you reach in to get them. Before grabbing your gerbil outright, stick your hand into the cage and let your gerbils get used to your smell. Stick your hand into the cage slowly, and let your gerbils come to your hand. After your gerbils begin to sniff you and become interested in your hand, begin to stroke their

The more you handle your gerbil, the more comfortable and relaxed he will feel about being held. Once your pet learns to trust you, he should be willing to climb into your hand from his cage.

backs softly. Do not pull your hand away too quickly. Sudden movements frighten gerbils. If you are going to allow children to hold your gerbils, watch them carefully. Children sometimes hold gerbils too tightly. This causes gerbils to squirm, which, in turn, causes children to squeeze even harder. Squeezing can cause serious injury to gerbils.

Never pick up a gerbil by its tail. Gerbils' tails have an interesting defense mechanism. When picked up by their tails, the tails can detach. In the wild, this is how some gerbils escape from predators.

If your gerbils show no interest in your hand, put a yummy treat in the palm of your hand. This will definitely get your gerbils' attention. To help

Treats are a good way to encourage your gerbil to climb onto your hand.

your gerbils feel comfortable, you can also speak to them in a soft, calm voice. This will help them become accustomed to you. Once the gerbil is comfortable in the palm of your hand, cup your other hand around it and lift the gerbil up. Do not be surprised if the gerbil licks or nips at your hand. Gerbils might not like being handled at first, but after a few tries, your gerbils will begin to trust you more. The more you handle gerbils, the more accustomed they will become to being handled. Over time, your gerbils should not mind being handled at all. Just be careful not to drop your gerbil—any fall could hurt a gerbil.

Once your gerbils are comfortable in your hand, you can begin to allow them to play outside their cage in a gerbil-proof room. Softly pet their backs, but let your gerbils scamper away if they want to. Forcing your gerbils to stay in the palm of your hand will cause the gerbils to associate your smell with a bad experience, and your gerbils might avoid your hand the next time.

READING A GERBIL'S BODY LANGUAGE

Gerbils communicate through body language. Once you become familiar with this type of communication, you can better understand your gerbils. Chattering teeth is a sign that a gerbil is angry. A Gerbil's teeth chatter when it gets into a fight or when anything else irritates it. If you notice your gerbil's teeth chattering, carefully return it to the cage by itself and give it time to calm down.

When a gerbil becomes excited or anxious, he may begin pounding both hind legs on the ground, producing a loud drumming sound. This is known as "thumping," and is another way that gerbils communicate. Thumping is a gerbil's way of warning others that danger is near. Gerbils may also thump at each other to signal arousal before mating.

Gerbils blink to show affection and to show their submission to other creatures. A gerbil that is licking your hand or its cage is trying to communicate that it is

FAST FACT

If your gerbils have gotten used to you and then suddenly begin to act afraid of you, wash your hands and try to pick them up again. Your gerbils recognize your smell, not your face, and some perfumes and body lotions can mask your natural scent, making you seem like a total stranger.

Through observation, you'll come to understand what your gerbil wants and develop a closer bond with your tiny friend.

thirsty. If your gerbils are licking, check their water bottle. If the water bottle is full and functional, your gerbils may have just wanted to give you a kiss.

EARNING A GERBIL'S TRUST

Your gerbils will be much more likely to trust you if you provide them with a safe, clean, and fun home. As with any living creature, having a nice home relieves a lot of stress. If ger-

bils do not have stress, they are more likely to befriend humans.

Another way to keep your gerbils calm and free of stress is to establish a routine for them. If you establish a routine, your gerbils will know what to expect, and they will not cower when you approach their cage. You can alert your gerbils that you are approaching by speaking in a sooth-ing voice, sticking your hand in their cage, and allowing the gerbils to come near you. These are all good ways to put gerbils at ease.

Most importantly, to build your gerbils' trust in you, you should never do something that could scare or hurt them. Several positive experiences will show your gerbils that their home is safe and secure. Once your gerbils realize that they do not have to worry about predators or danger, your gerbils will be ready to give you all their love and affection.

CHAPTER SIX

Gerbil Health Issues

Although gerbils are hardy animals, they do require medical attention in some situations. A veterinarian who specializes in rodents is the best person to assess a gerbil's health. Finding a veterinarian who treats small animals can be difficult. Some local veterinarians do not have the training to treat gerbils. You should talk to breeders in your area to find out who treats their gerbils. Pet suppliers may also have information on suitable veterinarians. If you are

Gerbils are relatively healthy pets, and probably won't need much in the way of veterinary care. An annual checkup by your vet is a good idea, though.

still searching for the right veterinarian, call a local humane society or animal shelter to see if they have any recommendations.

Your rodent veterinarian should see your gerbils for annual checkups. If this veterinarian is located far away, you should check to see if any small animal doctors in your community are willing to treat rodents in an emergency. Gerbil illnesses can become serious very quickly, so you might need to take your gerbils to someone nearby. In this case, you can have the local veterinarian contact the rodent veterinarian with any questions. Be sure to talk to both veterinarians about this situation before an emergency arises. You will also want to learn some basic information about the people who treat your gerbils. Find out how many rodents the veterinarian sees each month. Ask if your veterinarian has ever performed surgery on a rodent. If you do not plan on breeding gerbils, you might

also want to find out if the doctor has the training necessary to neuter or spay your gerbils.

It is important to visit the veterinarian when your gerbils are in good health. You should transport your gerbils using the same carrier or travel box you put your gerbils in while you are cleaning their cage. You should place the gerbil carrier

Not all veterinarians are trained or willing to treat rodents. Before an emergency arises, do some research to find a local veterinarian who is capable of treating your gerbil.

on the floor of your car. Make sure the carrier cannot fall and does not move much during the car ride. Travel can stress gerbils, so you should make the trip as comfortable as possible. Give your gerbils a drink, or a treat like a grape or a piece of pear, before the veterinarian sees them.

During the veterinarian's examination, explain your gerbils' normal behavior, their habitat, and their basic diet. This will help the veterinarian assess your gerbils' health. You should also tell your veterinarian if you intend to breed your gerbils. This will give the vet a better understanding of your gerbils' daily life. With any luck, your gerbils will need to visit the veterinarian only for their annual checkup. Still, certain situations require expert attention.

PREVENTING HEALTH PROBLEMS

Caring for your gerbils properly is the best way to prevent health issues. Your gerbils need a clean, stimulating environment to remain healthy and happy. Cleaning the tank regularly and introducing new toys from time to time will help keep your gerbils content. A properly balanced diet and easy access to water are also necessary for your gerbils. Check the tank daily to ensure that the temperature is comfortable. You should also

change the water in the water bottle daily. You can easily spot a potential problem if you take time each day to do a gerbil health check. Healthy gerbils have bright, clear eyes and smooth, shiny fur. Their fur should not be matted or dirty. They should be active and curious. Each one's nose should not be red or runny. They should have a good appetite, and their bellies should always be dry. You should listen carefully to make sure that your gerbils are breathing normally. A healthy gerbil does not click, sneeze, or wheeze. Examine the gerbils' droppings to make sure that they are firm and brown. If you notice any deviations, your gerbils may be suffering from one of the following common ailments.

COMMON GERBIL AILMENTS

ALLERGIES: A gerbil that has a red or runny nose with no other symptoms might be allergic to its litter. You can try switching to another litter first—preferably dust-free litter. If this does not solve the problem, your gerbil may have an infection that requires a veterinarian's attention.

DETACHED TAIL AND DEGLOVING: Gerbils' tails are detachable, so you should never hold or grab a gerbil by its tail. A detached tail will never grow back. If your gerbil's tail

A gerbil that isn't feeling well will appear lethargic and may have half-closed eyes. His fur may also appear matted and wet, rather than soft and shiny. If your gerbil starts to exhibit any of these symptoms, call your veterinarian immediately.

becomes detached, your gerbil will live. Put some antibiotic ointment on the end of the tail. You should observe your gerbil carefully for the next few days to make sure the tail does not become infected. If this happens, you will need to take your gerbil to the veterinarian. A degloved tail means that part of the skin has

come off, leaving the muscle of the tail exposed. This looks unpleasant, but it is not usually a problem. The exposed area will dry out and fall off after a few days. If this does not happen, or if you suspect the tail is in danger of infection (if a piece of bedding appears stuck to it, for example, or if there is exposed bone), take your gerbil to the veterinarian as soon as possible. The veterinarian may have to amputate part of the tail.

INFECTIOUS DISEASES: Bacteria, protozoa, or viruses usually cause infectious diseases. These diseases spread easily from one animal to another. Only a veterinarian can determine the exact cause of an illness, so it is best to take your gerbils to the doctor as soon as you recognize symptoms of an infectious disease. Of course, the best way to avoid exposing your gerbils to these illnesses is to practice good husbandry. Always wash your hands before handling your gerbils. You can also prevent disease by keeping your gerbils' tank clean and free of any contaminants. Always throw away uneaten food before it has a chance to spoil. Germs from rotten food will spread easily to your gerbils.

RESPIRATORY INFECTIONS: Respiratory infections are easy to recognize. Any clicking, wheezing, or labored breathing is a sign of respiratory distress. You might also notice that your gerbil's fur is puffed or that its eyes are half-closed. Colds can quickly turn into a respiratory infection, especially in young gerbils. The best course of action is to take your gerbil to the veterinarian immediately. Your veterinarian will most likely prescribe a course of antibiotics to treat the infection.

TYZZER'S DISEASE: Tyzzer's disease is an incurable bacterial infection that can cause death if it is not treated immediately. Symptoms include watery diarrhea, listlessness, and rapid health decline. Healthy gerbils contract Tyzzer's disease through direct contact with infected gerbils. The disease can also spread through contact with an infected gerbil's litter or bedding. Although antibiotics can help treat gerbils with Tyzzer's disease, there is no cure. If you are a breeder and your gerbils contract this disease, you

FAST FACT

Kinked tails and fixed wrists are two of the few genetic defects associated with gerbils. Although these conditions will not prevent your gerbil from living a long, healthy life, you should not breed gerbils with these defects because the trait is handed down to offspring.

must stop breeding from this line. You should also never place infected gerbils into new homes.

DENTAL PROBLEMS: Signs that a gerbil may have a dental problem include difficulty eating and weight loss. Your gerbil might also experience excessive salivation or a nasal or eye discharge. If you notice that your gerbil's teeth are overgrown, ask your veterinarian to trim them. A gerbil with broken or missing teeth will need softer foods to eat. You might consider feeding it cooked oatmeal or applesauce until the teeth grow back.

EAR AILMENTS: If you notice your gerbil tilting its head to one side, it may have a cyst or an inner ear infection. Older gerbils are prone to cysts of the ear. Although they are untreatable, these harmless growths do not

usually affect the gerbil's daily life. Inner ear infections are serious and require treatment by a veterinarian. If you notice your gerbil walking in a circle, it may be suffering from this condition. These infections can lead to a loss of balance and cause the gerbil to hold its head at a strange angle. The veterinarian will most likely recommend a course of antibiotics to treat the infection. Inner ear infections can incapacitate your gerbil and even lead to death, so it is best to seek immediate treatment.

KIDNEY DISEASE: If you notice your gerbil losing weight, refusing to eat, or becoming increasingly sluggish, your pet may be suffering from kidney disease. Older gerbils are especially susceptible to these infections. There is no treatment for these conditions, but you can help prevent kidney disease by feeding your gerbil a proper diet and providing easy access to fresh water.

INJURIES FROM FIGHTING: Even an established pair of gerbils can become aggressive toward each other and start fighting. You can treat small cuts at home with antibiotic ointment, but your veterinarian should attend to severe injuries. The more pressing issue is the change in your gerbils' behavior. You may want to

If your gerbil appears to be losing weight or is refusing to eat, there could be a problem with his kidneys. Call your veterinarian if he exhibits these symptoms, as they may be signs of a serious problem.

GERBIL EMERGENCY KIT

You should always keep some emergency supplies on hand in case anything happens to your gerbils. Your gerbil emergency kit should include the following items:

- Contact information for your veterinarian, a local animal hospital, and an all-night veterinary clinic (if there is one in your area)

- Antibiotic ointment

- Ornacycline antibiotic, which can be found in pet stores

- An eyedropper or medicine dispenser for emergency feeding

- A reptile warming lamp and bulb

- A hot-water bottle

have your veterinarian examine both gerbils to rule out an underlying medical condition. Sick or stressed gerbils may lash out at their companions. You should make sure your gerbils are kept in a quiet area of the house.

Your gerbils' cage may also be contributing to the problem. Carefully consider the size of the tank. You may want to purchase a larger tank to meet the needs of your gerbils. This could help reduce your

FAST FACT

The AGS recommends keeping extra gerbil food and litter on hand at all times in the event of a weather emergency or a power failure.

pets' stress levels and prevent any future fighting. If your gerbils continue to fight, you should reintroduce them using the split tank method described in Chapter 4.

LUMPS AND BUMPS: While some lumps and bumps may be the result of an injury, tumors could be the cause of others. Tumors are more common in older gerbils. They start out as a small growth on the skin. Bleeding and infections can occur if the tumor continues to grow. It is best to have tumors examined by your veterinarian. The veterinarian can determine if surgery is necessary to remove the growth.

SEIZURES: Scientists estimate that about 20 to 40 percent of all gerbils

Sometimes, surgery is required to remove a tumor from a gerbil's scent gland. This photo shows a gerbil getting anesthesia before surgery. Such procedures are challenging because of a gerbil's tiny size and delicate frame.

suffer from seizures. During a seizure, a gerbil will lie rigid and motionless on the floor of its tank. Some gerbils will jerk uncontrollably before collapsing. These events usually last for a few minutes. After the seizure, the gerbil resumes its normal behavior. Seizures have few long-term effects and do not reduce the gerbil's quality of life. You should not breed gerbils that suffer from seizures. Many believe this condition is genetic and is passed down to the offspring.

STROKES: If you notice that your gerbil is limping, it may have suffered a stroke. Another indicator of stroke is paralysis on one side of the body. If you think your gerbil has suffered a stroke, make sure it has easy access to food and water. After a few days, most gerbils who had a stroke return to normal. Some may have a permanent limp and move slowly. There is no treatment for strokes. If your gerbil appears to be in pain or cannot eat or drink after a stroke, you should take it to the veterinarian. Euthanasia may be the only humane option at this point.

CARING FOR A SICK GERBIL

Depending on the illness, your sick gerbil may require some extra care. You should keep your gerbil in a warm, quiet area. You do not want your gerbil to experience any stress while it is recovering. Consider placing a heating pad or a reptile heating clamp lamp outside the tank for extra warmth. Install a thermometer on the outside of the tank to monitor the temperature. If your gerbil has difficulty moving, make sure it has easy access to food and water. Carefully follow all directions when administering any medications prescribed by your veterinarian. You should not attempt to treat any complications on your own.

If your gerbil's condition changes or worsens, contact your veterinarian immediately. It is not a good idea to separate your gerbils when one of

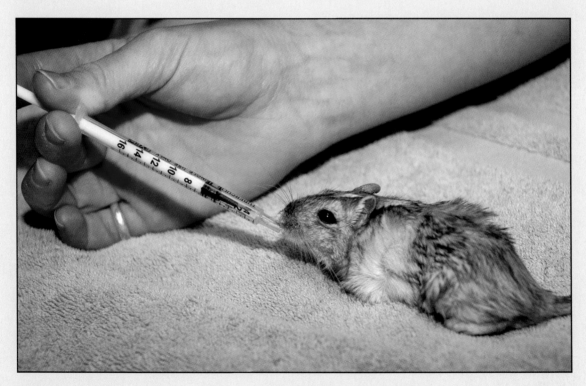

Pets that are ill are more likely to become dehydrated, which compounds their health problems. You may need to use a medicine dropper to make sure that your gerbil is getting enough to drink each day.

them is ill. If one gerbil contracts an illness, the other gerbil will most likely need treatment. Separating your gerbils can be stressful, and it is often difficult to put them back together once the sick gerbil has recovered. The gerbils may fight and hurt each other once they return to the same tank. You may wish to separate your gerbils, however, if one is recovering from surgery. Ask your veterinarian if it would be safe to use a split cage (see Chapter 4) so the gerbils are still next to each other.

Remember to keep the tank clean, especially if your gerbil is recovering from surgery or fighting injuries. A clean environment helps reduce the risk of a secondary infection. When it comes to caring for your gerbils, there is no substitute for proper nutrition and good husbandry. Quality care from the start can help your gerbils live long, healthy lives.

CHAPTER SEVEN

Enjoying Your Gerbils

You will be happy to learn that your gerbils are one of the most easily entertained pets. A simple shoebox cave or the leftover tube from a roll of paper towels can keep these curious rodents occupied for hours. This chapter discusses a number of ways that you can entertain and enjoy your gerbil. You will undoubtedly come up with some other creative ideas on your own, though.

ENTERTAINING YOUR GERBILS

During their playtime, your gerbils will want to run free. Gerbils enjoy

Watching a gerbil explore his enclosure can be very entertaining.

the chance to escape from their cages and explore the outside world. Letting your gerbils run free, how- ever, does not mean giving them free rein of your house. Your house is full of gerbil hazards, such as

Gerbils may enjoy playing with some of your toys in addition to their own. Just be sure to keep a very close eye on them to ensure their safety.

electrical wires, heating vents, air-conditioning vents, drains, and other hiding places. You should never allow your gerbils to run around outside. Gerbils can encounter harmful parasites and pesticides in the grass. Your gerbils should spend their free time in a hazard-free, escape-proof room. To gerbil-proof a room, set up a barricade or simply close the door and block any potential escape routes, such as spaces under doors, heating vents, and cracks. Then allow your gerbils to explore their new surroundings. Always supervise your gerbils during their out-of-cage excursions to keep them safe. During your gerbils' free time, you should lock away any other pets. You should also keep in mind that your gerbils will relieve themselves anywhere, so you may not want to let them roam free in an area with nice carpeting. Slippery, smooth floors, however, can be a hazard to your gerbils. When gerbils get tired, they will often return to their cage on their own. Consider leaving your gerbils' cage open and accessible so they can return to it when they are ready. When gerbils feel frightened, they like to hide. During their time outside their cage, provide them with some hideaways such as a box, a cardboard tube, or a paper bag.

Gerbils enjoy running free to get exercise, but they have a natural desire to gnaw, burrow, climb, and run. A few inexpensive, or even homemade, toys will give your gerbils the opportunity to engage in these activities. The best gerbil toys are made of untreated wood. Wooden toys are perfect for climbing and gnawing. A simple wooden block with some cutouts serves multiple purposes. Gerbils can hide in the holes, chew the wood, and climb on the block. A wooden ladder provides similar entertainment and may even serve as access to the cage door after a fun session of running free.

Cardboard boxes and tubes might not seem like much fun to you, but they are an amusement park to your gerbils. You can tape a few boxes together to construct a staircase for your gerbils to climb. Cut holes in the boxes to create

FAST FACT

If your gerbils live in a complex cage with many tunnels and hideaways, it is a good idea to teach them a cue so they will come to the door. This will make it easier to remove them when you need to clean their cage.

dark caves and hideouts. Build a maze for your gerbils by connecting numerous boxes and tubes. Divide your gerbils' tank in half with a piece of cardboard and watch as your gerbils try to maneuver over, under, or around the fence. The best thing about these homemade, cardboard toys is that when gerbils get tired of them, they will gnaw them to pieces and build comfortable nests to nap in.

Another one of gerbils' favorite activities is running. Both exercise wheels and run-about balls will keep your gerbils in shape. The best exercise wheels for gerbils are made of solid metal and have no spokes. A traditional hamster wheel with openings between the wires can be dangerous for gerbils because it can catch their tails as they run. You can modify a traditional hamster wheel by lining the inside of the wheel with cardboard. Keep in mind, however, that gerbils may chew on the cardboard; if so, you will need to replace it periodically. Plastic wheels are available, but your gerbils will likely gnaw on the wheel, and plastic is harmful to gerbils if they ingest it. If your gerbils live in a wire-frame cage, when choosing a wheel, look for one that attaches to the side of the cage; if they live in a tank, choose a wheel that can be tied or

fastened to the lid of the tank. These wheels are more stable than the free-standing ones, which can tip over and injure your gerbils.

Run-about balls serve as an alternative to exercise wheels. A run-about ball is a hollow ball with air vents and a door. To use a run-about ball, simply place a gerbil inside the ball and close the door. Set the ball on the floor and allow your gerbil to run wherever it wants to go. Run-about balls give your gerbils exercise and freedom at the same time. Always supervise gerbils when they are inside run-about balls. Keep them off tabletops and away from staircases and doorways. You should also watch for signs of overheating. Even well-ventilated run-about balls can get very warm in a short time. Never allow your gerbils to spend more than fifteen minutes at a time in a run-about ball. When playtime in the run-about ball is over, return your gerbil to its cage, and clean the ball thoroughly, both inside and out.

To give your gerbils even more fun and excitement, you can turn their cage into a playground. As described in Chapter 5, you can give them a dust bath filled with chinchilla sand. Your gerbils will burrow and roll in the dust. This will also clean your gerbils. You can add a wooden see-saw and watch your gerbils test their

Gerbils just love to run, so putting an exercise wheel in their cage will help them burn off excess energy. However, the wire kind pictured here is not necessarily ideal for your little friends, as their tiny paws tend to slip between the bars while they are running. A solid plastic wheel would be a better option.

strength and balance. By securing a crumpled, paper grocery bag to the side of your gerbils' tank, you can create a mountain for your gerbils to climb.

You can also entertain your gerbils without spending a dime. Snap your fingers, tap the tank side, hum, or whisper. Your curious gerbils will search for the source of these myste-rious noises. Another no-cost activity for your gerbils is exploring your sleeves. Put on a shirt with long, loose sleeves and allow your gerbils to explore. They will likely crawl up and down your arm to find their way through this interesting new tunnel.

While you certainly want your gerbils to live happy, healthy lives, you do not want to overwhelm

Who says your gerbils need expensive pet store toys? Your gerbils will have just as much fun navigating a shirt sleeve or pocket. While their curiosity may be cute, you must remember that your friend is delicate, so play gently.

FAST FACT

A gerbil's teeth continue to grow through-out its life, so it is important for your gerbils to have plenty of materials to gnaw on. Untreated wood is a gerbil favorite!

them. A wooden block or two, an exercise wheel or two, and some burrowing material are all they really need to stay entertained. Do not overload your gerbils' home with toys and gadgets. You should also avoid buying plastic toys, such as hideouts or blocks. Gerbils like to gnaw, and gnawing on plastic can harm them, especially if they swallow the pieces.

LETTING YOUR GERBILS ENTERTAIN YOU

Playtime for your gerbils is not only fun for your gerbils—it is also fun for you. They will make you laugh as they climb in and out of boxes or roll around the floor in their run-about balls. If you want your gerbils to be even more entertaining, however, you can teach them to do tricks.

While your gerbils will certainly appreciate food rewards, they truly love spending time outside their tanks. After your gerbils successful-

ly perform a trick, give them some time to run free. Your gerbil will quickly learn to associate the trick with an excellent reward.

Use sound cues, such as taps or hums, to train your gerbils. To teach your gerbils to come, for example, place a wooden block near the cage door. Give the wooden block a few taps with your knuckle and then leave a special treat for your gerbils, such as a piece of fruit or some vegetables. It may take a few tries before your gerbils understand that they will get a reward when you tap on the block. After a few days, however, they will catch on and come to the wooden block to receive a treat as soon as you tap. At this point, give your gerbils the best of all rewards—time to play outside their cage. Allow your gerbils to play for a few minutes. Then place them back in the cage. When they move away from the block, tap it again, and wait for them to return. Allow them to spend another few minutes

FAST FACT

Gerbils love sunflower seeds. Use them as a special treat when you want to teach them a new trick.

running free. Before long, your gerbils will race to the block as soon as you tap.

Teaching your gerbils to beg is easy. Start by holding a treat, such as a peanut or a pumpkin seed, above their heads. The gerbils will have to sit up to reach the treat. Each day, hold the treat slightly higher until your gerbils have to stand on their hind legs to reach the treat. From then on, whenever your gerbils see your fingers above their heads, they will stand up and beg.

Your gerbils can also learn to jump into your hand. To teach this trick, place your gerbils on top of their cage. Hold a treat in your hand just beneath the edge of the cage. After your gerbils hop into your hand, allow them to eat the treat and have some time to run free. Before long, your gerbils will want to hop into your hand from almost any location. Just make sure you do not place your hand in a position that might lead your gerbil to fall. Falls are dangerous for gerbils.

If you use your imagination, you can probably think of many tricks to teach your gerbils that will keep you entertained for hours. Try teaching your gerbils to run a maze, ride on your shoulder, or balance on your arm like tiny circus performers.

ARTISTIC GERBILS

Some gerbils climb; some gerbils burrow. Phoebe, a gerbil owned by Judith and Stuart Block, created art. The Blocks purchased Phoebe at a pet store in New York City. At the time, they did not know that the newest member of their family was an artist at heart.

Phoebe began her sculpting career in May 2003. Throughout her short life, she managed to create ten unique sculptures with names such as "Desert Dreams," "Sunset on the Gobi," and "Antler Totem." Phoebe carefully crafted each sculpture from thick, colorful, cardboard tubes. Even though Phoebe passed away, her art continues to live on.

If you think your gerbil has some artistic ability, let it run through some nontoxic paint and create a masterpiece on paper. For a less messy art project, fold a piece of paper several times and allow your gerbil to nibble on it to create paper snowflakes. Better yet, toss your gerbil a thick, cardboard tube and see if it is the next gerbil sculptor extraordinaire!

TO LEAVE OR NOT TO LEAVE YOUR GERBILS

Every now and then, you may decide to get away and take a vacation. As a responsible pet owner, you will have to make accommodations for your gerbils while you are away. This may mean bringing your gerbils with you, hiring a gerbil sitter, or simply leaving your gerbils alone for a few days.

TRAVELING WITH YOUR GERBILS: If you decide to bring your gerbils along with you, remember that your relaxing vacation is actually stressful for your gerbils. Gerbils have trouble adjusting to new environments, which is why you should travel with them only when you are going short distances. You should also do your best to keep their routines and schedules as normal as possible while you are traveling. Gerbils can travel in their regular cage unless it is too large or intricate to safely transport. When traveling with your gerbils, remember to bring extra supplies.

You will need food, water, a water bottle, extra bedding, and any toys or accessories that keep your gerbil happy and occupied. Everyday upkeep of your gerbils' tank is necessary when traveling. Be sure to remove and replace wet or soiled bedding and to clean your gerbils' home as often as necessary.

As you travel, it is important to make sure your gerbils get enough water. Rather than dealing with a leaky water bottle on the road, you

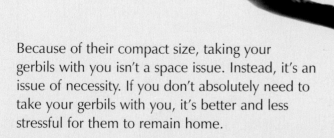

Because of their compact size, taking your gerbils with you isn't a space issue. Instead, it's an issue of necessity. If you don't absolutely need to take your gerbils with you, it's better and less stressful for them to remain home.

should give your gerbil a treat with a lot of water in it, such as a small piece of pear or a grape. When you make stops on your journey, temporarily attach the water bottle to your gerbils' cage so they can quench their thirst if they want to.

When traveling with your gerbils, place the cage in a secure location in the car. One of the safest places is on the floor. Placing the cage on the seat is a bad idea because it could slide off the seat during sudden stops or starts. Before hitting the road, you should remove the gerbils' wheel from the cage. Sudden twists, turns, and stops can throw your gerbil off balance when it is running on the wheel, which can cause injury. You should not leave your gerbils in the car for extended periods. Temperatures that are too hot or too cold are potentially harmful to gerbils and can lead to illness or death.

TRAVELING WITHOUT YOUR GERBILS: Taking your gerbils with you on a vacation or trip is not always an option. During short trips that last two or three days, you can leave your gerbils at home alone. Before you leave, prepare their tank with fresh bedding, extra food and water, and a few toys to keep them occupied. For longer trips, you will need to hire a pet sitter for your gerbils—or have a reliable friend, relative, or neighbor care for your gerbils in your absence.

The person who cares for your gerbils must be trustworthy—you are leaving your gerbils' lives in this person's hands. Before your trip, invite the sitter over and review your gerbils' daily schedules and routines with her. You should also leave detailed instructions near your gerbils' cage. Tell the sitter how much food to give to your gerbils each day. Explain how to fill the water bottle and attach it to the side of the tank. You should also leave your phone number and the phone number of

If you need to find a sitter for your gerbils while you're away, the Pet Sitters International Web site can be a valuable resource.

your veterinarian. Before you leave, clean the cage thoroughly. Tell the pet sitter when and how to replace wet or soiled bedding. Make it easy for her to check on your gerbils by placing their cages in the same room and leaving necessary supplies nearby. Explain the signs and symptoms of illness so she knows if the gerbils need a veterinarian. To maintain your gerbils' health and welfare, clean the cage thoroughly again after you return.

If you are unable to find a friend, a relative, or a pet sitter to care for your gerbils while you are away, check with local pet stores. Some offer boarding services and will provide your gerbils with proper care while you are away.

CARING FOR YOUR SENIOR GERBIL

Like all living things, gerbils will grow old. The maximum life span of gerbils is about three to five years. As your gerbils age, you may begin to notice some minor behavioral changes. Your senior gerbils may enjoy the same activities that they enjoyed as energetic youths, but they will become less playful and daring. They will still interact with other gerbils, but not as frequently. Because they are less active, you'll need to make sure that they do not gain too much weight. Give them plenty of time to run free to get exercise. You should try to feed them foods with less protein and fat.

Elderly gerbils run a greater risk of developing health problems than younger gerbils. Many begin to lose their ability to hear high-pitched sounds. They are also at a higher risk of developing tumors and cardiovascular problems—problems of

As your gerbils age, you may notice them slowing down just a bit. Don't worry, this is normal.

FAST FACT

Elderly gerbils do not gnaw as much as younger gerbils, which can cause their teeth to grow too long. A veterinarian can trim your senior gerbils' overgrown teeth.

the heart and blood vessels. To protect your senior gerbils from developing diseases, you should feed them a balanced diet, provide them with plenty of gnawing materials, and protect them from drafts, which can lead to colds.

Even with the best care, elderly gerbils may develop diseases and need medical attention. Some signs and symptoms will alert you that it is time to take your gerbil to a veterinarian. If your gerbil has a prolonged case of diarrhea, spends most of its time alone, avoids contact with the other gerbil in its tank or cage, loses weight, becomes less active or

AND THEN THERE WAS ONE

Gerbils are social creatures. It is best, therefore, to purchase a pair of gerbils of the same age at the same time. The two gerbils can play together, groom each other, and cuddle. Unfortunately, when one gerbil passes away, it leaves the other completely alone. Although we cannot know for sure, the remaining gerbil likely feels a sense of loss.

Rather than introducing just one young gerbil to cheer up your lonely senior gerbil, consider giving it two new playmates. The new pair of gerbils will give your elderly gerbil the comfort and companionship it needs. In addition, when this gerbil passes away, your two new gerbils will serve as a comfort to each other. Before you introduce new companions to your older gerbil, however, think about

whether your senior gerbil is easily stressed or especially prone to fighting. Perhaps it would be a good idea to talk to your vet before making a decision.

When you add new gerbils to your elderly gerbil's cage or tank, take care to integrate them properly. This will probably take more effort than introducing two young gerbils to each other. Wait until your senior gerbil has been alone for at least a week or two before introducing the new gerbils. Your elderly gerbil may not like having strangers in its home at first, but after a while, it will learn to tolerate them and befriend them. If your new gerbils are under ten weeks old and from the same litter, they are less likely to be territorial with each other, or with your senior gerbil.

Losing a pet is never easy. However, looking at photographs and remembering happy times after the pet's passing is a healthy way to help deal with grief.

responsive, or lies limp and exhausted in the corner of its cage, you should call the veterinarian. You should also make an appointment with the veterinarian if your gerbil's fur begins to look matted and unhealthy.

HOW TO SAY GOOD-BYE TO YOUR GERBIL

Throughout their short lives, your gerbils may become your friends, your travel companions, and a great source of fun and entertainment. Like all pets, however, your gerbils cannot live forever. Losing a pet is always difficult for a family. While adults may grasp the idea of the circle of life, children will likely struggle to cope with the loss of their soft, furry friends. They may need extra comfort and time to grieve.

Sometimes it helps to have a small memorial service for your gerbil. As you prepare to bury your gerbil, go through old pictures of your gerbil and share your favorite memories. Allow everyone in your family to express their feelings and say their final farewells. Understand that children may wish to return to the site of the burial on occasion to visit.

You should also do what you can to comfort your remaining gerbil. A lonely gerbil needs special attention and love to cope with the loss of its companion.

Organizations to Contact

American Animal Hospital Association
12575 W. Bayaud Ave.
Lakewood, CO 80228
Phone: 303-986-2800
Toll free: 800-883-6301
Fax: 303-986-1700
E-mail: info@aahanet.org
Web site: www.aahanet.org

American Fancy Rat and Mouse Association (AFRMA)
9230 64th Street
Riverside, CA 92509-5924
Phone: (909) 238-5231
Email: mcrattie@earthlink.net
Web site: www.afrma.org

American Gerbil Society
P.O. Box 1687
New York, NY 10159
E-mail:
donna.anastasi@agsgerbils.org
Web site: www.agsgerbils.org

American Humane Association
63 Inverness Dr. East
Englewood, CO 80112
Phone: 303-792-9900
Fax: 303-792-5333
Web site: www.americanhumane.org

American Holistic Veterinary Medical Association (AHVMA)
2218 Old Emmorton Road
Bel Air, MD 21015
Phone: 410-569-0795
Fax: 410-569-2346
Email: office@ahvma.org
Web site: www.ahvma.org

American Society for the Prevention of Cruelty to Animals
424 East 92nd St.
New York, NY 10128
Phone: 212-876-7700
E-mail: information@aspca.org
Web site: www.aspca.org

**American Veterinary
Medical Association**
1931 North Meacham Rd.,
Suite 100
Schaumburg, IL 60173
Phone: 847-925-8070
Fax: 847-925-1329
E-mail: avmainfo@avma.org
Web site: www.avma.org

**Association of Exotic Mammal
Veterinarians (AEMV)**
P.O. Box 396
Weare, NH 03281-0396
Phone: unlisted
Fax: 478-757-1315
Email: info@aemv.org
Web site: www.aemv.org

**Canadian Federation
of Humane Societies**
102-30 Concourse Gate
Ottawa, Ontario, Canada
K2E 7V7
Phone: 613-224-8072
Toll free: 888-678-CFHS
E-mail: info@cfhs.ca
Web site: www.cfhs.ca

Delta Society
875 124th Avenue NE, Suite 101
Bellevue, WA 98005
Phone: 425-226-7357
Fax: 425-679-5539
Email: info@deltasociety.org
Web site: www.deltasociety.org

**Humane Society
of the United States**
2100 L St., NW
Washington, DC 20037
Phone: 202-452-1100
Web site: www.hsus.org

**National Association of
Professional Pet Sitters (NAPPS)**
17000 Commerce Parkway, Suite C
Mt. Laurel, NJ 08054
Phone: 856-439-0324
Fax: 856-439-0525
Email: napps@ahint.com
Web site: www.petsitters.org

National 4-H Headquarters
U.S. Department of Agriculture
1400 Independence Avenue, SW,
Stop 2225
Washington, DC 20250-2225
Phone: 202-720-2908
Fax: 202-720-9366
Email: 4hhq@csrees.usda.gov
Web site: www.national4-h
      headquarters.gov

**Pet Industry Joint Advisory
Council**
1220 19th Street, NW Suite 400
Washington, DC 20036
Phone: 202-452-1525
Fax: 202-293-4377
Web site: pijac.org
E-mail: info@pijac.org

Pet Loss Support Hotline
College of Veterinary Medicine
Cornell University
Ithaca, NY 14853-6401
Phone: 607-253-3932
Web site: www.vet.cornell.edu/
      public/petloss

Pet Sitters International (PSI)
201 East King Street
King, NC 27021-9161
Phone: 336-983-9222
Fax: 336-983-9222
Web site: www.petsit.com

Further Reading

Anastasi, Donna. *Gerbils: The Complete Guide to Gerbils*. Irvine, Calif.: Bowtie Press, 2005.

Dew, Brian. *Pet Owner's Guide to the Gerbil*. Gloucestershire, UK: Ringpress Books, Ltd., 2001.

Feeny, Kathy. *Caring for Your Gerbil*. Mankato, Minn.: Capstone Press, 2008.

Fox, Sue. *Gerbils*. Neptune City, N.J.: T.F.H. Publications, 2007.

Holland, Laurie. *Gerbils as a Hobby*. Neptune City, N.J.: T.F.H. Publications, 1994.

Kötter, Engelbert. *My Gerbil and Me*. Translated by Celia Bohannon. Hauppauge, N.Y.: Barron's Educational Series, Inc., 2002. First published 2000 by Grafe.

Landau, Elaine. *Your Pet Gerbil*, rev. ed. San Francisco: Children's Press, 2007.

Page, Gill. *Getting to Know Your Gerbil*. Surrey, UK: Interpet Publishing, 2002.

Piers, Helen. *Taking Care of Your Gerbils*. Hauppauge, N.Y.: Barron's Educational Series, Inc., 1995.

Putnam, Perry. *Guide to Owning a Gerbil*. Neptune City, NJ: T.F.H. Publications, 1997.

Sikora Sino, Betsy. *The Gerbil: An Owner's Guide to a Happy Healthy Pet*. Hoboken, N.J.: Howell Book House, 2000.

Viner, Bradley. *All About Your Gerbil*. Hauppauge, N.Y.: Barron's Educational Series, Inc., 1999.

Internet Resources

www.egerbil.com

The eGerbil Web site offers many resources for gerbil owners and breeders. The Web site features an online store with books, DVDs, and other resources to help you learn about gerbils. The site also offers general information about gerbil nutrition, care, and housing. Articles and lists regarding certain species of gerbils are included on the site. The Web site instructs gerbil owners on how to complete do-it-yourself projects for their gerbil tank. It even features a forum where gerbil owners can talk to each other.

www.gerbils.co.uk

The National Gerbil Society is a British society that offers information about keeping gerbils as pets. Their Web site offers articles and frequently asked questions about gerbils. It also features photographs and descriptions of different species of gerbils. Also included is a searchable index of the topics that can be found on the Web site.

www.hannas.com/srg

The Shawsheen River Gerbils Web site offers information about gerbil care. The Web site also features rescued gerbils that are available for adoption. A unique feature of this Web site is the Gerbilpedia, a user-created section of facts about gerbil care and housing. The Web site also contains frequently asked questions about adopting gerbils from rescues.

www.petfinder.com

PetFinder is a valuable resource for those who are considering adopting gerbils from a shelter or rescue organization. Specify your location and search for gerbils under the "Small & Furry" option to see a list of all the gerbils available for adoption near you, with their names, ages, genders, and photographs. All participating shelters and rescues on the site offer contact information.

www.rmca.org

Although this Web site is sponsored by the Rat and Mouse Club of America, it may be a valuable resource for gerbil owners. The Web site includes care sheets and information about rodents. It also provides a list of rescues and shelters where rodents can be dropped off or adopted. The Web site also offers its members a list of veterinarians who treat rodents.

www.thegerbils.com

The Gerbils Web site offers a variety of information for gerbil owners and people thinking about getting gerbils. The Web site features a frequently asked question section that is very useful for gerbil owners. It also contains care sheets and information about raising your gerbils. The Web site also includes information about adopting gerbils, as well as pictures and videos of gerbils.

www.twinsqueaks.com

The Twin Squeaks Gerbils Web site offers care sheets and information about gerbils and their habitats. The Web site features monthly tips, which give gerbil owners ideas about cost-effective toys and housing solutions. The Web site also contains a "Just for Kids" section with games and activities. This section helps kids understand their responsibilities and jobs as gerbil owners.

Index

Numbers in **bold italics** refer to captions.

Contributors

REBECCA SPARLING is an editor for Northeast Editing, an educational book production company. She graduated from Marywood University with a Bachelor of Arts in English. A lifelong animal lover, Rebecca grew up in southern New York, where she helped her parents care for everything from spoiled cats and pampered pooches to injured hawks and abandoned raccoons. Her current four-legged companions are several rescued cats that rule the office where she works. In her spare time, Rebecca enjoys reading, crocheting, and spending time outdoors. Rebecca lives in Northeast Pennsylvania with her husband, Paul.

Senior Consulting Editor **GARY KORSGAARD, DVM,** has had a long and distinguished career in veterinary medicine. After graduating from The Ohio State University's College of Veterinary Medicine in 1963, he spent two years as a captain in the Veterinary Corps of the U.S. Army. During that time he attended the Walter Reed Army Institute of Research and became Chief of the Veterinary Division for the Sixth Army Medical Laboratory at the Presidio, San Francisco.

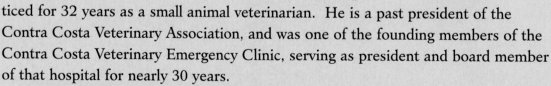

In 1968 Dr. Korsgaard founded the Monte Vista Veterinary Hospital in Concord, California, where he practiced for 32 years as a small animal veterinarian. He is a past president of the Contra Costa Veterinary Association, and was one of the founding members of the Contra Costa Veterinary Emergency Clinic, serving as president and board member of that hospital for nearly 30 years.

Dr. Korsgaard retired in 2000, and currently enjoys golf, hiking, international travel, and spending time with his wife Susan and their three children and four grandchildren.